THE THREE HOUSES is a work of nonfiction. Some names and identifying characteristics have been changed to protect the privacy of the individuals.

For more information visit **www.kcsd.ca**

FIRST EDITION

ISBN#: 978-1-7772913-0-3 (Paperback)
ISBN#: 978-1-7772913-3-4 (Hardcover book)
ISBN#: 978-1-7772913-2-7 (Audio)
ISBN#: 978-1-7772913-1-0 (Electronic book)

Printed in Canada

Cover Design by Nipun Kasote, Joss Monzon, and Kulbir Colin Singh Dhillon.

Book designed by www.kloman.ca

Kulbir Colin Singh Dhillon

The Three Houses

Kulbir Colin Singh Dhillon

DEDICATION

To my best friend and the grounding wire in my life, Satinder (Cindy), our love provides us both with nutriments for healthy living. To my son, Pavitar, and daughter, Veerah, you both are by far my best creations. I hope you continue to flourish and become worthy citizens of this global village.

To my parents, Rashpal Singh and the Late Gurbaksh Kaur Dhillon. Your dedication and commitment to truth, spirituality, and doing the right thing are foundational to the person I am today. To my parents in Canada, Balbir Singh and Nirmal Kaur Bassi, you have both been loving parents. Thank you for your unconditional support.

"You have every right to walk around with a chip on your shoulder, but you don't...Why? That is why you need to share your story, write a book," he said. None of this would have become reality if not for the encouragement and mentorship of Michael 'Pinball' Clemons. I thank you for inspiring me and thousands of others. Thank you, brother.

Lastly, shout out to all the dreamers and glass-half-full types; the kind of people that make 'giving' an essential part of their daily lives. The born sevadars (those individuals that perform selfless service for humanity) that provide a smile, a helping hand, advice, and always give something...for they have understood the secret to a better life!

FOREWARD

My gentle celebrity has afforded me the opportunity to brush up to brilliance more often than I deserve. It is my belief that the GIANTS in our community who give out of scarcity proliferate our culture. Yes, the bold, gentle souls who have the audacity to give more than they have to give. Many argue logically that's impossible, that's because they've never seen it. However, our author is not that. Colin Dhillon is accomplished but uncomfortable, balanced but begging for more, by all measures successful but unsatisfied. COMPLICATED!

Actually, kind and complicated. The first time we met for dinner, I can't remember the restaurant or our culinary choices because the conversation was so rich and palatable. As we unpacked his truth, personal success was not enough! He has this insatiable desire for others to arrive and thrive. Colin is this uncanny combination of energy and old spirit. He has so much to give, so much to say and so much to share. Discovering the breadth and depth of his lived experience, I urged him to write a book. From growing up in England, before brown was welcome in town to his meteoric rise in corporate Canada; he poignantly reveals the strength in the struggle and the rewards of endurance. A teacher at heart, this gift of prose unveils three principles of life: contentment, commitment, and contribution.

This structure consistently gives way to his electric personality that introduces a randomness to his work. With help in every chapter, this book is replete with commercials of culture, combined with stories of faith, mental health, and racism, complemented by flashes of randomness at the close of each chapter. Be it faith, family, or finance it's not enough for our author to win, he wants the same for you! A common man with uncommon compassion!

Mr. Dhillon, our meeting is now my treasure, and I'm confident the readers will feel the same.

Love, Respect and Admiration,

Michael "Pinball" Clemons
CFL and Canadian Sports Hall of Fame

CONTENTS

LIST OF ILLUSTRATIONS

RANDOMNESS: A LIST OF VERY SHORT STORIES

PREFACE

My name is Kulbir Singh Dhillon, but known to my world as Colin Dhillon. I was born a dreamer. My father was an Artist and a Teacher, my Grandfather was a Headmaster, and my mother was a feisty and fearless left-handed snake killer. Their DNA was their gift to inspire me after it created me.

Humans have been storytellers ever since the advent of speech. An early ancestor may have described acts of cunning and bravery to his enraptured loved ones, as they sat in dim-lit caves with a low, smouldering fire before them. Others may have laughed or rolled their eyes while listening to the stories under a *Wild Syringa* tree in the African plains. They watched similar adventures brought to life by being pantomimed by a different forefather. However, the event that unfolds is over in the blink of an eye. Remembering how it all played out gives it a breath of life. The value that it carries in bringing lessons learned to other scenarios is what gives it body and form. It is the animated energy that supports a story that truly brings it to life. Stories share emotions and intimate feelings with those that choose to read, listen, or watch the play unfold. We, as readers or viewers, cannot help but become emotionally connected, sometimes becoming actors in the game itself. Our sacred texts become a compilation of stories, bringing us closer to our point of origin directly and viscerally.

I am a British Sikh. I grew up in the West Midlands, in a town called Tipton. I would think my story isn't that different from those that grew up in the 1960s and 70s as British Asians. I am a creative individual, one who has always been a dreamer and a constant learner. My design-thinking and persistence have led me to be able to surpass some of my perceived career and life goals.

Today, I am the CTO, whose job is to help launch connected and autonomous vehicle technology in the Canadian automotive sector, and a founder of Project Arrow; Canada's introduction into the zero-emission vehicle (ZEV) industry. I speak globally by challenging the automotive industry norms, stimulating those that choose to listen, elevating their thinking, and more importantly, their actions (doing). I am also the Chairman and Co-founder of the Sikh Heritage Museum of Canada, a charitable organization dedicated to advancing and promoting the understanding and preservation of the cultural and religious life of the Sikh community.

I am obliged to share my story with those that know me and those of you who don't. Though I may seem to live an average mundane life, my world is far from ordinary. My daily life is both beautiful and enriching for the soul and mind. "How?" you might ask. "It's all in the mind". I often say that I live a blessed life, and lives and situations are created within you, and then reflect outwards around you. If it's sunny on the inside, it most likely won't be cloudy and grey on the outside! I was nine years old when I first heard about the Bayeux Tapestry. A 230-foot-long embroidered piece of fabric that tells the story of the Norman conquest of England (Norman, Flemish, Breton, and French people). This linen piece consists of colourful renditions of battles and events surrounding the invasion. I share this because I am and have been a student of history for many a decade and because my life and this book have been like a tapestry, where millions of colourful silk and wool yarns are replaced with incidents and occurrences that collectively complete this piece of art.

Although my stories and life journeys may bring laughter and tears, and evoke a range of emotions, my underlying hope is to inspire souls as much as I can. To empower and uplift you, urging you to live a life of fulfillment and to never feel defeated, no matter how defected you might think you already are.

We all have stories to share. Some follow a path that takes us home as far back as we can go to our ancestral history and origins, pointing out scenarios and persons of significance along the way. Some are anecdotes of events from our recent past that give a colourful relevance to the moment that absorbs us. Trickles and waves of emotions felt and expressed by both the teller and listener reflect the contents of the story and the relationships between both. The storyteller transforms and transcends him/herself through the sharing of the personal journey. The narration provides a different lens through which their experiences are viewed. For me, my stories allow me to learn about myself indirectly. My stories are my gift. They help me understand my past and to provide a *virtual* bridge to the future. I have been on a personal journey for over forty plus years of my life. For a large portion of this time, I did not realize that I was like an astronaut in the deep dark universe; I travelled in solitude with my thoughts, dreams, and visions being my closest companions for long periods.

I am artistically inclined and a design thinker. I dream in colour, especially when I am awake. I use analogies to help paint them. I see ideas in my mind, and they usually appear in three-dimensions. The blooming thoughts grow into clear visions, and I sometimes feel like a spectator in my head. In my work, I need the assistance of symbols, pictograms, and icons to help explain to others the ideas that are part and parcel of my daily dreaming.

How do we make sense of the banality of the daily grind? We try to see it in different shapes and contexts and apply it to ourselves and each other. I picture us going about our daily lives, much like hamsters running on an endless wheel. We tend to consume ourselves with a desire to be in constant motion, trying to make as much sense of our world as possible, but isn't there more to life?

Humans have an innate drive to ask questions and seek answers. The drive applies to our everyday problems and situations, but more importantly, to the journey that we are all a part of. My journey has led me to question the extent to which the average human suffers. I am not talking about those brothers and sisters living through warfare, mass starvation, natural disasters, or crippling diseases, but rather the non-physical pain. I mean psychological pain where one feels overwhelmed with negative thoughts and feelings of misery. I, like most of us, naturally empathize with our neighbours and fellow humans. How much of our suffering can be categorized as self-inflicted, and how much is inherited Deoxyribonucleic acid (DNA)? Perhaps, we add layers of anguish to our life experiences, just like adding inches to our waistlines without plan or intent, one guilty morsel at a time? Before we know it, the layers have added up to a collective culture of suffering. If we are not mindful of our outlook, we can become mired in situations that are painful and would remain in that dark state, unable to pull ourselves out. We can also choose to understand the situation as short-lived and focus on finding the good in it, or the lesson in the moment and make plans to move past it.

I perceive our daily circumambulations on the wheel happening in three pieces, one nesting inside the other like Russian *Matryoshka* dolls. All three are integral and internal to each other; the greater physical form is manifesting within the smaller being. Just as there are millions of species, so too there are millions of universes. I will eventually invite you to enter the realm of *The Three Houses.*

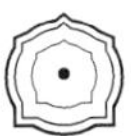

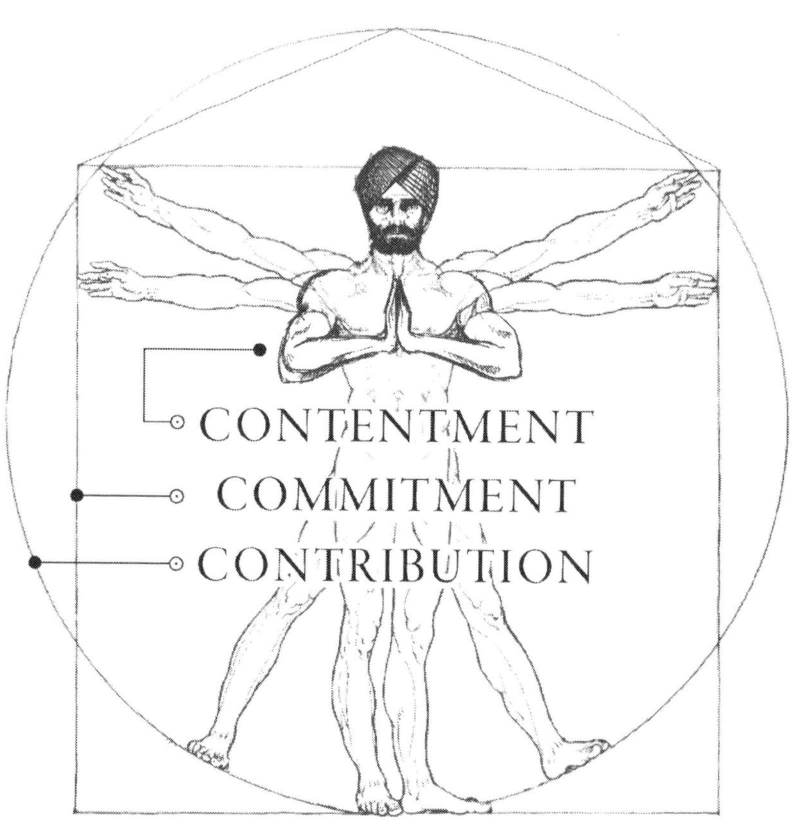

Illustration 1: The Three Houses
by Kulbir Colin Singh Dhillon

This journey called *life* cannot possibly be enjoyed to the constant refrain from the back seat of "are we there yet?" Instead, we must rise and take charge. We need to savour the journey and be in control of every situation that arises to divert our focus. The imagery rushing into your mind as you look outside the window of your speeding life needs to have colours, textures, and contrasts deciphered and taken in with a quieter intensity. Scene by scene, moment by moment, and before we know it, the projected images from within becomes a sub-story, and the plot that materializes in one's mind becomes the start of an epic journey of the imagination. I am expressive and passionate about everything I do, and it comes from having a window seat on this spectacular ride.

"Without imagination and an inner resourcefulness, you are but a shade of grey"

- Kulbir Colin Singh Dhillon

NAVIGATION

Yes, this is a historical list of accounts throughout my life, but it is not a memoir. Rather, it is a non-fictional book that shares my spiritual, social, and creative journey. Some stories may be deemed pious, and others will border on being politically incorrect - they are all stepping stones of experience and elements of my personal growth. They are milestones and flag posts in the timeline of my life. Most of these accounts occurred while I was a young chap, and I am thankful for experiencing them all. They helped mould me to become the man that I am today.

All my life I have been breaking stereotypes, willingly and unwillingly. I am blessed to be on an awakened spiritual journey for most of my life. Some people will go through their entire life without connecting to their spiritual core, and for those that do have this inclination, they get placed upon a pedestal, sometimes revered by others, be aware that at some point in your life, you will be toppled and smashed into thousands of pieces. The shattered remnants will possibly make it hard to identify who or what sat on top of that plinth. Instead, let's not fall into that trap of placing the so-called religious or spiritually inclined individuals on these pedestals. Instead, let's kick the spiritual platforms away, try to find our own Personal Jesus (Depeche Mode song. 1989), and liberate ourselves as we continue to make mistakes and grow as individuals.

This book has three sections: **The Foundation Years, The Building Years,** and **The Décor.** The analogy is of a building and its progress, from laying a solid foundation to completion and adornment of both the interior and exterior.

As you work your way through the book, I hope you will experience a variety of emotions. Welcome to the ride, it may be bumpy at times and *unconventional* at others, but I anticipate you will enjoy both the journey and its scenery. You will also find short stories scattered throughout the book called "randomness". These stories are short bursts, anecdotes through my eyes that help to keep the overall concept of this book flowing in a slightly dysfunctional manner. They also reflect my mode of communication…always sharing anecdotes to support a narrative. I have decided to use quotes from multiple sources, some of which are religious and spiritual, others from people who have simply obtained a level of notoriety and are known to the masses. Each quote is aimed at providing both substance and support to the subsections that dwell within.

The Three Houses is the journey of an individual who feels destined to share his life's voyage in hopes of inspiring and uplifting the reader. I had every opportunity to carry my baggage of the adversity I experienced, but I chose against it. I will happily share my modus operandi. I identify myself as being an average person, yet my life, both internal and external are filled with some of life's greatest gifts. These are the experiences I will share with you in this textual journey for a better life.

Kulbir Colin Singh Dhillon

THE FOUNDATIONAL YEARS

Illustration 2: Gospel Oak Road, Tipton. UK
by Kulbir Colin Singh Dhillon

CHAPTER 1

Born n' Bred in the Black Country

In this Black Country, including West Bromwich, Dudley, Darlaston, Bilston, and several minor villages, a perpetual twilight reigns during the day, and during the night, fires on all sides light up the dark landscape with a fiery glow. The pleasant green of pastures is almost unknown, the streams, in which no fishes swim, are black and unwholesome; the natural dead flat is often broken by high hills of cinders and spoils from the mines. The few trees are stunted and blasted; no birds are to be seen, except a few smoky sparrows; and for miles on miles a black waste spreads around, where furnaces continually smoke, steam engines thud and hiss, and long chains clank, while blind gin horses walk their doleful round. From time to time, you pass a cluster of deserted roofless cottages of dingiest brick, half- swallowed up in sinking pits or inclining to every point of the compass, while the timbers point up like the ribs of a half-decayed corpse. The majority of the natives of this Tartarian region are in full keeping with the scenery – savages, without the grace of savages, coarsely clad in filthy garments with no change on weekends or Sundays, they converse in a language belarded with fearful and disgusting oaths, which can scarcely be recognised as the same as that of civilised England.

- Samuel Sidney, Rides on Railway - 1851

Who am I? I'm a British Sikh. I was born in 1970 in a town called Tipton, England. I now reside just outside of the Metropolis called Toronto in a rural village known as Caledon. I live a blessed life, hallowed even, yet my personal journey will not read or unfold without the many bumps, awkward moments, and odd bruises. Like all life journeys, I had the choice of taking two paths; the low road to personal oblivion, and nowhere, and the high road to personal freedom - from the shackles of society, religious doctrine, and innate insecurity.

I am a thinker and mind-mining creator. Part of my subconscious responsibility is to simplify the complex; make ideas and dreams tangible. As I nurture my thoughts, I help to apply the right environment for them to grow and become sustainable.

The analogy of a seed planted in dark, fertile soil is a perfect visual to use for the growth of a fragile mind. The outer projection of life helps the seedling develop deep roots from which it matures. Everything it needs to establish trickles down through the dirt. It absorbs nutrients, stretches, and expands to break free to reach its full potential.

My fertile dirt was aptly called the Black Country. It got the name sometime during the middle of the mid-1800s when it was the hub of British heavy industry.

Legend says that Queen Victoria christened it the Black Country due to the hundreds of chimney stacks spewing thick black smoke into the darkening skies.

In trying to convey the town's atmosphere and surroundings, there is only one word that comes to mind...dull. Tipton was excruciatingly, painfully, and endlessly grey.

"Don't judge each day by the harvest you reap but by the seeds that you plant."

- Robert Louis Stevenson

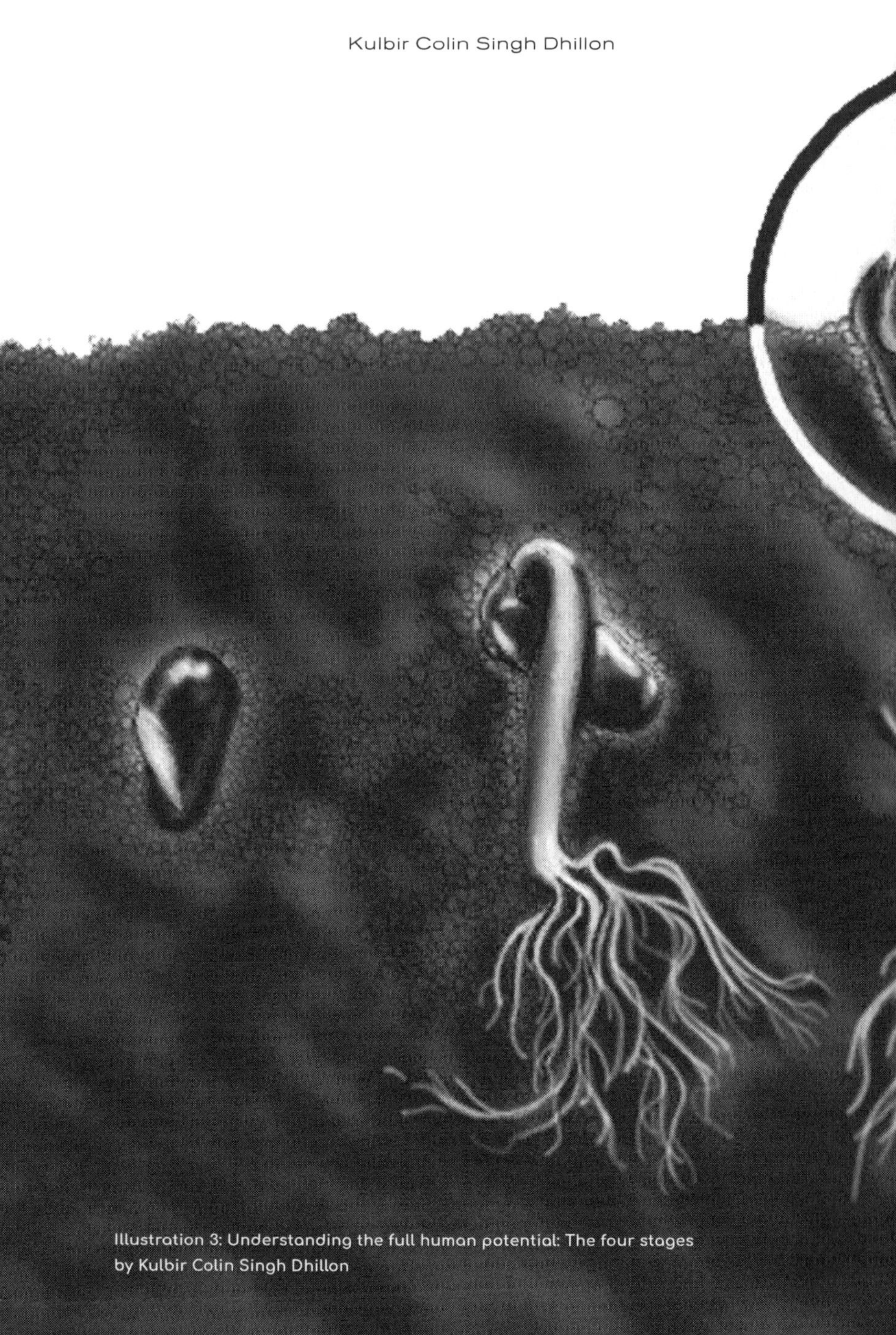

Illustration 3: Understanding the full human potential: The four stages
by Kulbir Colin Singh Dhillon

The Three Houses

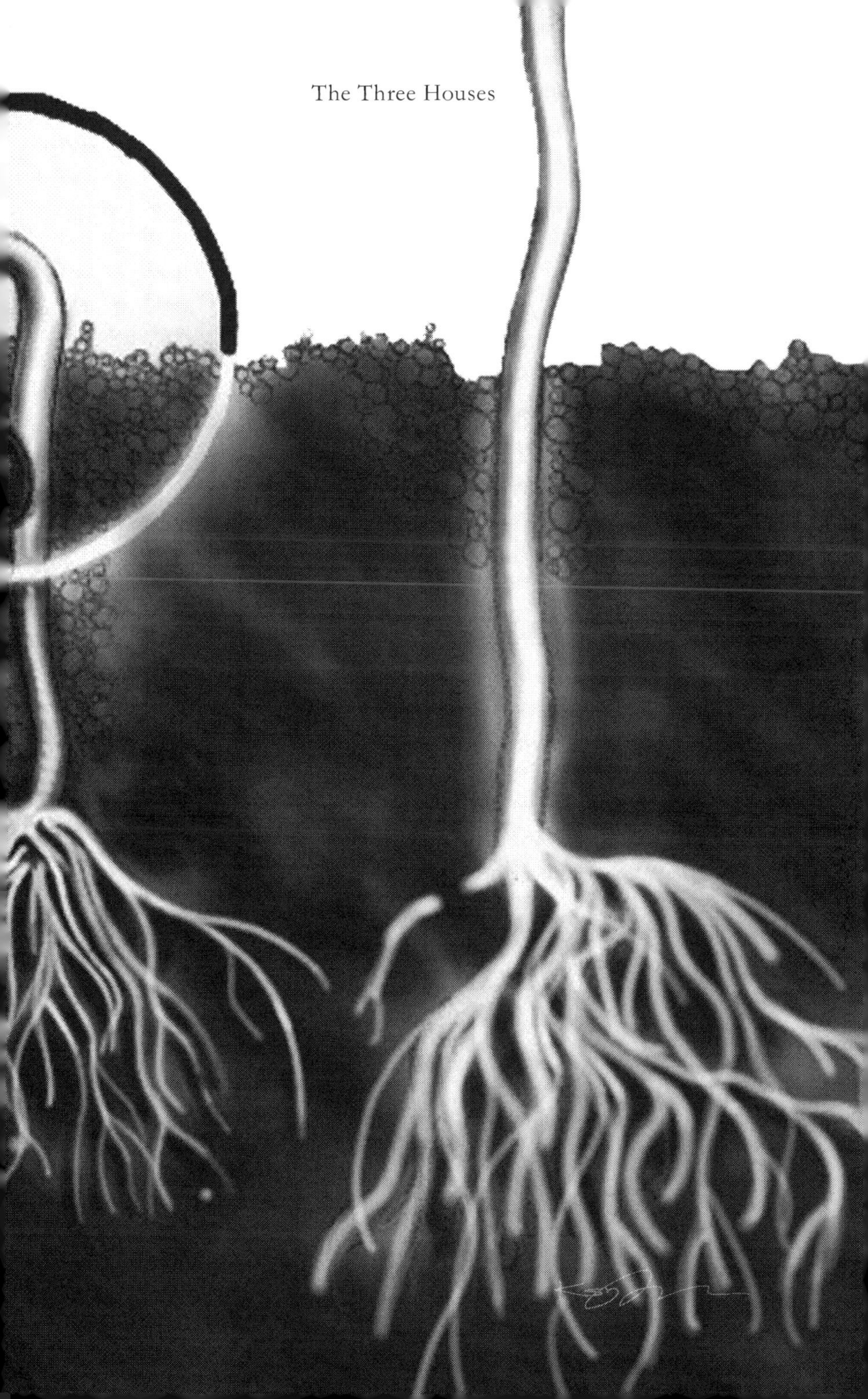

The 1970s was the decade that finally placed the last *forged* nail in the coffin of the Industrial Revolution in the Black Country. Though the chimneys and stacks were no longer spewing black smoke, the dull grey aftermath remained in the gloomy, bland faces of the people, populating our monotonous, dismal town. These words might sound harsh and the brush stroke might be classified as being too broad, yet I am generalizing, trying to paint a picture with a limited colour palette.

Though I was brought home from the hospital to a house on Bloomfield Road, where we shared a home with my Dad's two other brothers and their families. The house I remember while growing up was on Gospel Oak Road. This Victorian terrace house provided many of my early childhood memories, like hearing my Dad and his younger brother (Chacha) talk about 'Ali' and how great he was. They talked about how nobody was able to beat him (the small black and white television was up on a shelf, and they stood around watching the fight as I wandered by). The Ali I am referring to is Muhammed Ali, and the fight was his third fight against Ken Norton, which took place on the 28th of September 1976.

This house, like many built in the same era, had no washroom facilities inside the house. To use the toilet, you would need to go outside, and a bathtub or shower was non-existent. I remember seeing my dad working with the contracted builder in the room behind the kitchen; the coal room. He decided to convert this into a three-piece washroom, even though his neighbours said he was mad. "Why would you want to bring the toilet inside the house?" they said…well maybe because we no longer wanted to urinate into a piss pot and have to venture outdoors for a number two! I vividly remember the four-by-four-inch white ceramic tiles, the white tub, and the galvanized steel tub that hung behind the kitchen door. Before the washroom was completed, the typical bathing routine occurred on a Friday evening. The galvanized tub would be placed on the kitchen floor and filled with both water from the tap and boiled water from the whistling kettle. One by one, we, the children of the house, were given our weekly bath (another British custom). I was the third eldest of four children in the house…I'm pretty sure I stood in the tub of water used by both my brother and cousin! I could still feel the good-old English, cold damp air penetrating my dank wet self.

Like many other Punjabi Sikh immigrants, my parents left their country of origin to arrive on the shores of this cold island. Why? Well, to earn money! India was under British Imperialism rule from 1858 onwards. Before that, it was under a Corporation; a Company that was ruling India from around 1757. The British East India Company began to trade with the ruling *Mughal* Empire and Princely kingdoms in the early 1600s. In 1670, the English monarch, King James II, provisioned the British East India Company with a series of acts, giving them so-called rights to:

- Autonomous territorial acquisitions.
- Mint money.
- Exercise both civil and criminal jurisdiction over areas.
- Command fortresses and troops.
- Make war and peace as they saw fit.

The self-styled traders had fast become invaders with an eye on monopolizing this land called *Bharat* (India), and the roadmap to doing so was through the network of princely states and kingdoms. Similar to Europe in the 1800s, this was a divided, self-centred landmass, not a united nation. The coastal trading cities were the first to go. The last vestiges to fall were *Punjab, Delhi, Oudh, and Rajasthan.*

A commercial company enslaved a nation comprising two hundred million people.

- Leo Tolstoy, Letter to a Hindu, 14 December 1908.

The Sikh Kingdom (*Punjab*, from where my parents and ancestors resided) today would have included parts of India, Pakistan, Afghanistan, Tibet, and bordering China. Not only would it be a land of great wealth and a major military powerhouse, but also significant from a geographical standpoint. Founded in 1799, the Sikh kingdom provided civil liberties to all of its people. An education budget surpassed England before "true education of the *Panjab* was crippled, checked, and was nearly destroyed and the opportunities for its healthy revival and development were either neglected or perverted." (History of Indigenous Education in the Panjab since Annexation and in 1882, by G.W Leitner). Let's just say... perverted!

The death of its visionary one-eyed leader, *Maharajah Ranjeet Singh* in 1839 was followed by the ill-appointed heirs to the throne and continuous onslaught and betrayal of the highest order by the British with the *Misl* (Clan) leaders and courtesans, thereby allowing the Sikh kingdom to prematurely fall. Two Anglo-Sikh wars were fought. The outcome of the second Anglo-Sikh War (1848 - 1849) gave the British both the Sikh Kingdom and the strategic control of the whole of *Bharat.*

540 - 327 B.C.	Western Punjab part of the Persian Empire
327 – 325 B.C.	Alexander (Sikander) of Macedonia
325 – 303 B.C.	Western Punjab part of the Seleucid [Greek EMPIRE
303 – c. 180	B.C Punjab part of the Mauryan empire Chandragupta Maurya, Ashoka spread of Buddhism
180 B.C – 10 A.D.	Western Punjab under the Indo-Greeks Menander. Antial-cidas
0	Foundation of Lahore by Lah, Lava, Loh or Low, son of Rama
30 – 385 A.D.	Punjab part of the Kushan empire
120 - 146	Huvishka, Kanishka
606 - 647	East Punjab under Harsha visit of Hiuen Tsang, Chinese pilgrim
999 - 1195	Ghaznavid and Ghorid dynasties Mahmud Ghaznavi
1195 - 1526	Afghan and Turkish empires in North India
1469 – 1539	Guru Nanak Dev Ji
1526 - 1540	First phase of Mughal empire with Babur, Kamran Mirza, Humayun
1540 - 1555	Suri Dynasty. Fort of Rohtas
1555 - 1799	Punjab part of the Mughal empire
1577	Foundation of Amritsar
1588	Foundation of Harmandir
1799 - 1849	Sikh Kingdom
1845 - 1849	Anglo Sikh War I & II
1849 - 1947	Punjab under British Rule
1947	Punjab annexed (Pakistan & India)

Table: Chronology of Punjab History by Kulbir Colin Singh Dhillon

India was but one of the many countries that were under British rule. The Empire included many dominions, colonies, and territories. What were once trading posts now covered a quarter of earth's total land area and one-fifth of the world's population at the time (458 million, the clear majority of those being in India). Racism and prejudicial attitudes were stewards of the Empire. Though you may be a citizen of the Empire, your skin colour and nationality may have restricted your movement and any chances for permanent residency. Indians wanting to immigrate to those lands occupied by European descendants were heavily regulated to the point of being barred. The *myth* of Empire existed for the clear majority of its coloured residents... Queen Victoria's 1858 proclamation concerning India and its people was an empty promise. Though she stated, "We hold ourselves bound to the Natives of our Indian territories by the same obligations of duty which bind us to all our other subjects". It was obvious that somebody forgot to send out the memo!

Most Indian immigrants, of my parent's generation, had plans to return home when they had earned enough money in the UK. Sufficient amounts to buy more land and property, and to make purchases of new mechanical equipment to work their land, enough to lessen the physical hardship of farming and ease their later years. Enough to nourish the land so that it became more profitable and plentiful. Their effort would rejuvenate the property so that it would provide wholesome, golden grains that would yield comfort and wealth when their bodies began the inevitable decline as they aged. This was the intent of my parents, but my arrival might have changed all that.

I was born on Sunday, October 4, 1970, to *Rashpal Singh* and *Gurbaksh Kaur Dhillon*. I was their second son. My elder brother, *Rajesh*, the noble Prince of our clan, was born in India 2 years earlier. The day of my arrival must have been a proud and joyful day for everyone, beyond the norm. I was the first child in the *Dhillon* clan to be born outside of *Punjab*, India. A garden makes a home, and I was their first seed to germinate in the fertile black soil of the British Empire. The golden fields they had left behind would be tilled by others while they tended to their new crop. My father reminded us on many occasions, "We only stayed here in England because we knew the education and employment opportunities for you both would be better." He would say this with a five-pound note raised above his head, in his right hand. They put their backs and hearts to work that plot of excruciatingly, painfully, endlessly gloomy dirt to something better, all so that we could thrive and have better lives.

If I close my eyes and let the film reel roll, it would loosely resemble a parental guidance movie, telling the story of a determined individual with tough residences on more hardened streets. You would walk them, dodging a clear, unobstructed flow of racism. You were pelted with it daily. Grandparents, parents, and children wearing dodgy 70s fashion apparel would curse you with expletives as rough and coarse as the denim they wore. For those struggling to visualize my description, Stephen Frears' 1985 movie, *'My Beautiful Launderette,'* captured the dreariness of it all, quite well as did Damien O'Donnell's *'East is East'*. We became used to the feeling of being the only family of colour in predominantly white neighbourhoods. My brother and I would be the only turban-wearing *Sikhs* in both the junior school and high school we attended. These experiences, through the late 1970s and 1980s, were tough "character building" exercises, to say the least. On odd occasions, when we complained to our mother of the bullying and difficulties we faced as turban-wearing *Sikhs*, her response, which echoed my father's *Game of Thrones* style speech, was that we don't understand the real value of the crown *(turban)* we wear today and that we would later in life. To which I whispered in my brother's ear, "that's if we are still alive mate!"

We had to navigate the practice of our faith in a virulently Christian culture. It was made trickier because our experience of *Sikhism* was filtered through our parents explaining the religion, its rituals, and customs to us. The Christians were not practicing, even if they were very staunch at proclaiming their religious status. High unemployment rates made it easier for some parts of the country to simply point fingers at the visible minorities as the reason for their growing poverty and joblessness. It was much more fulfilling to single us out rather than question the government's policies on their inability to keep existing manufacturing within the boundaries of the United Kingdom. Race relations and racism as a sub-culture festered, especially in areas of high unemployment. Tipton was smack-bang in the ground zero of one of those deprived zones.

The 1970s and 80s were a turbulent time for the British economy and its immigrants and offspring. Britain in the 1970s: *Troubled*

Economy, edited by Richard Coopey & Nicholas Wood-ward and *Britain in the Seventies – Our Unfinest Hour? By Kenneth O. Morgan* both describe how Britain had plummeted into the dark ages, and the 80s were a challenge for not only immigrants but those marginalized in society under Prime Minister Margaret Thatcher.

This backdrop will build one's character or send you so deep into a rabbit hole that your real personality might never see the light of day. Many of the first-generation British Asians *(Sikhs)* like me were about to proceed over the socioracial 'bed of coals' as we entered educational institutions surrounded by the social turmoil. Who appears, or should I say... if we appear, on the other side was yet to be seen?

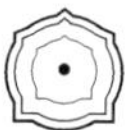

The Three Houses

Randomness:

INDIAN TRADERS-TO-NORDIC VIKINGS-TO-SIKHS?

Where are you from? NO, like where are you actually from?

This is a question I have been asked numerous times. The question implies that I am from another place other than the United Kingdom or Canada, when in fact I am British born.

Well, how about if I replied, "from Finland"?

After a recent DNA test, it was discovered that 8% of my father's DNA comes from the Nordic region, specifically Finland, 1% from the United Kingdom, and 1% from North America's original people; the indigenous people.

The more Science and Technology continue to break open the traditions and steadfast views of many, the closer I would assume humanity can come together.

The more society begins to challenge the inequality of ALL its people, the more I would assume humanity can come together.

The more time we as individuals, couples, parents, and guardians spend in learning about one another and how we have more in common, the more I would assume humanity can come together.

So, my ancestors originate from the Indian subcontinent. Others come from the Nordic region, Europe and North America. This DNA soup is served up for the global village citizens...be proud of your heritage, but let's not get carried away folks!

image: www.ancestry.com graphic (2018)

Photo: Great Bridge Primary School (1978/9)

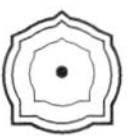

CHAPTER 2

Bob Dylan's Brother

My Father, *Rashpal*, was the second son of *Harkrishan Singh Dhillon* from the village *Sagarpur, Punjab. Harkrishan* was a Headmaster and a philanthropist who built many a village school, to help facilitate education for girls and boys, and *Gurdwaras* (Sikh house of worship) accessible for all. He was the Headmaster at *Phagwara, Pasla, Bilga, Rurkui, Khothran, Shahcote, Gumtala,* and *Nurmahal* high school, *Jallandhar* district from the *Doab* (A Persian word which means between two rivers. The *Doab* in *Punjab* is between the *Sutlej* & *Beas* rivers). My Dad was one of ten siblings; four boys were born, followed by six strong, beautiful girls.

We are from the Dhillon **Jatt* clan that traces their lineage back 4,000 years, to the time of the Hindu God, Lord *Krishna.* The legend of the Dhillon name is traced back to a king called *Karna*. He was the eldest son of Queen *Kunti*, the aunt of Lord *Krishna.* These characters are all part of the great epic poem, the *Mahabharata.* The Dhillon's are also known as *Raja Jatts* (*Raja* means King and *Jatt* means Landowner), as a large number of this clan sat on the throne of *Delhi* (which is actually a derivative of the word Dhillon).

My Grandfather kept a diary that traced the family lineage right back to King *Karna*. When he shared the contents with his children, there was generally a politely muttered, "Well, isn't that something?" to accompany the discrete eye-rolling. You see, very few believed it to be true. The diary was passed on to my father after Grandad's passing. Years later, I was on one of my frequent trips to India when I was approached by a man who had just discovered that my last name was Dhillon. He validated my Grandfather's claim when he greeted me with the statement,

I cocked my head to the left and raised an eyebrow, a physical reaction of surprise that I inherited from my Mum.

"All Dhillon's should know of their rich heritage and lineage traced back to a great warrior. King *Karna* had a reputation for being a pious, generous man. Did you know that we Dhillon's have sat on the throne of India more than any other clan?"

---

*Originally from Central Asia, the Jatts are an ethnic group from the Northern parts of India and Pakistan. Jatts were designated in a British report as a "Martial Race", which was a designation created by officials of British India to describe "races" that were thought to possess qualities such as courage, loyalty, self-sufficiency, physical strength, resilience, orderliness, hard-working, fighting tenacity, and military tactics.

I was thrilled to find that my Grandfather's claim was not only verbally validated but expanded upon. The Dhillon's that I knew shared some commonalities, for sure! They had a tendency to stand with their head and shoulders back as though blue blood coursed through their veins or a pickle of some substantial size had been inserted into that place where the sun don't shine! The natural bearing that came across as being a wee bit arrogant seemed to have some historical reasoning behind it, which I was happy to find.

The stories of my Mother's childhood are equally legendary, if not steeped in the same noble warrior history. She was born in the state of *Punjab* but brought up in *Uttar Pradesh (UP)*. My Mother did not conform to the expected behaviours of a girl growing up in the 1950s. The cosmic class of British and Indian social etiquettes and nuances must have been brutal to those that didn't fit the cookie-cut moulds. She defied stereotypes and marched to the tune of her own drum *(dhol)* in an atmosphere where adherence to societal expectations was customary and deviation was punished. There was a large Muslim population in the region she was raised in, which perceived and discriminated against left-handers (the right hand was used in Indian and middle eastern society for eating with. The left-hand was used to clean your backside). If a student was caught writing left-handed, they were soundly thrashed. She was left-handed and I guess I might have inherited that mendelian trait from her. She had a reputation for being headstrong, abrupt, and fearless. At a very young age, she became known as The Snake Killer.

Mum was about 12 years old one summer when her mother went into the grain storage room to find a *King Cobra coiled on a pile of wheat. She slammed the door shut behind her as she ran out screaming. Then, a messenger was sent to track down my mother. Even though she was the youngest of seven children (four boys and three girls), it was my mother who was called to deal with the snake. Her siblings stood by as she fearlessly tackled the challenge. She opened the door to the storage room and looked in to assess the danger. Then, she closed the door again. When she came back, she had her trusted bamboo stick in her hand and a nervous household for an audience. She whipped the door wide open and stood tall with her feet shoulder-width apart in battle stance at the threshold. With both hands gripping the bamboo stick, she began to slowly move it in a rhythmic motion, which can be described to resemble the figure 8. The King Cobra responded by flaring its hood and swaying along to my mother's movements. When the stick and the snake synchronized their deadly dance to the same thudding heartbeats, my mother lunged. She aimed her blows for the snake's head. Her aim was true, and she emerged from the storage room dragging the snake out by its tail. She was met by the household and many of the local villages celebrating her victory. My mother, not even a teenager yet, walked through everyone with a stick in one hand and a snake in the other and made a dry comment on their lack of courage. The legend still lives on!

---

*King Cobra: is a large venomous snake found in India and other parts of Asia. It can grow up to eighteen feet in length and has enough toxic venom in its bite, to kill an elephant.

I was given a good *Sikh* name by my parents at birth. *Kulbir*. '*Kul*', meaning 'ancestral descendants' and '*Bir*', meaning 'great protector'. The name *Kulbir* conveys my duty to act as a protector of a great rich heritage.

In September 1976, after moving from Gospel Oak Road to Napier Drive in sunny Tipton, a change of schools was also in the cards. I was moving from Ocker Hill Infant and Nursery School to Great Bridge Primary School, which was going to be our centre for learning until graduation when we would be vaulted off to the big leagues at Alexander High School. The whole experience of starting a new school was nerve-wracking for a six-year-old. The thought of entering an unknown environment with strange faces and smells was daunting. Until we moved into our new home, my Mum walked my brother *Rajesh* and me partway to school, to Toll End Road. She would go in one direction from there and walk to work, while *Rajesh* and I would walk fifteen minutes in another direction to get to school. We were only six and eight years old!

I was grateful to have a layer of armour to help me through the changes; My maternal uncle, who I called *Mama Ji* had visited from Canada the year before. He brought my brother a pair of jeans and a matching jean jacket. Thankfully, they didn't fit *Rajesh*, so I got them. I was excited to be able to have an outfit in which I could start school looking like my television idol, the *Six Million Dollar Man*.

See, at this moment in life, I don't remember feeling different from other children. Yes, my skin complexion was a few shades darker than the average. The colour of my hair was black, not blonde, brown, or ginger. My Dad drove a British Rover P6 3500s car like other respectable dads did. The worst thing that I had ever done was lay down in the middle of our street, right on top of the white staggered line, with a cousin who will remain nameless. This act eventually got us into trouble. All of the kids, whether brown, black, or white, we had our faults and our differences, but deep down inside, we all wished that we were bionic and that made us more alike than different. We made the same sounds emanated from our voices with no accent to identify our ancestral origin. We ran together in slow motion, oblivious to the differences that would matter so very much in only a short time. We were just two of only a dozen Indian children in the entire school. The social demographics of the neighbourhood highlighted a high rate of unemployment. The high cost of labour was driving business offshore and Tipton was not an affluent town to begin with. Economic circumstances will have a differing effect on people. Differences between groups of people, whether religious or ethnic, are barely visible during times of prosperity. The same differences become charged with the possibility of violence when people have to fight over the perception of dwindling resources. At the time, Northern Ireland was exploding due to *The Troubles.* In the 16th century, England placed prominent Protestant nobles right into Holy Catholic, Ireland. Fast forward a few centuries, and Ireland agitated for its independence using forcefulness, similar to what occurred in

India. "Sunday bloody Sunday". In the 1960s and 70s, the IRA (Irish Republic Army) was at war with Britain, and the daily news showed images that were bloody and derelict. Tipton and the rest of England were blanketed by this conflict, and it affected the psyche and attitudes, provoking nationalism, and here I was, the son of an immigrant.

On a Monday morning, Dad set off with my brother and me to Mount Street. We were off to the school office at Great Bridge Primary to start a new educational chapter and to meet our new Headmaster, Mr. Dalhousie. He was a tall man and had a real sense of presence about him. He was balding with tufted islands of hair on either side of his head. Large rimmed glasses magnified his striking and authoritative eyes. His smile was special. Mr. Dalhousie was a man of faith. A six-year-old was not about to comprehend this but there was a reassurance about him that was palpable, even to a child.

"Well, Mr. *Dhillon*, I was thinking", he said to my father who stood tall, flanked by my brother and me, outside the doors to the main school building.

"To help the boys assimilate into their new school, I was thinking why we don't call *Rajesh* *'Bob' and *Kulbir* 'Colin'? Having names that are easy to pronounce would make life much easier for the boys, the fellow students and our teachers, no?"

---

*My Brother was called Bob after the legendary Bob Dylan.

My Dad looked down at both of us. "It's up to the boys to decide." He said.

I remember looking up at my Dad and then at my brother. A fleeting glance at Mr. Dalhousie and then back at my Dad. I was six and my brother was eight. We were oblivious to mass culture and the names sounded short and easy. We nodded in agreement. We were now *christened* Bob and Colin *Dhillon*. The legacy of that moment has lasted well into the present. There was a point in the mid-90s when I attempted to eliminate the anglicized name, but the change never really took hold. Eventually, I gave in and now, I embrace the name Colin and integrated it into my given name as *Kulbir* Colin *Singh Dhillon.*

There was most definitely a practice of anglicizing foreign names of individuals and places by the Brits. Culturally, it goes back to the Medieval ages when names in Latin or classical Greek were modified. It was a practice for Immigration officials to *tweak* the name, or at least the spelling when new immigrants arrived on the shores. One can argue that it was supported by Christian beliefs too. Mr. Dalhousie was a good Christian. He would quite often pull out his acoustic guitar and play the tune to a hymn or a song written about Jesus. I have always wondered why he did not suggest the idea of just shortening our names from *Rajesh* to *Raj* and *Kulbir* to *Kul.* Truth be told, how difficult is it to read and pronounce our names? They both have two syllables and phonetically, let's be honest, they roll off the tongue too.

Maybe if my relationship with Mr. Dalhousie would have been different from what it actually was, I might have dropped the Colin tag, but honestly, Mr. Dalhousie was an important figure and somebody that I felt was supportive of both *Rajesh* and myself, and the fact that our parents were not offended allowed us to still use Bob and Colin today.

Randomness:

THE GOLDEN TICKET TO WONKALAND.

In 1962, the Conservative British Government introduced the first Commonwealth Immigration Act, a law that was aimed at limiting the number of immigrants arriving into Britain from the Commonwealth countries, such as India and Pakistan. Hugh Gaitskell, the leader of the opposition, called the act the anticolour legislation. So going forward, immigration was greatly restricted, too much colour from the global palette was gonna mess up the British mixing dish. Now, individuals wanting to arrive on the shores of Britain would need a work voucher. This voucher was graded according to the applicant's employment prospects. The vouchers could be obtained through family members already happily employed, doing those mundane jobs that some folks thought were below them, even though it needed to be supported by a company willing to provide employment. My Father's Director at Brickhouse Foundry was called Alf. He was the man that signed the vouchers, thereby allowing them to work and live in England.

A Christmas didn't pass when the brothers didn't get together and would go to Alf's home to drop off a gift and to say their annual thank you for the golden Wonka tickets!

MINISTRY OF LABOUR Ref. No. [redacted]

VOUCHER

Issued for the purposes of Section 2 of the
COMMONWEALTH IMMIGRANTS ACT, 1962

IMMIGRATION OFFICER (30) 14 AUG 1963

Voucher Nº 045410 Date of Expiry [redacted]

See Extension Overleaf

CHITWAL

Full Name [redacted]

Address [redacted] DIST.HOSHIARPUR, PUNJAB, INDIA.

Date of Birth [redacted] Sex M/F Country of Birth INDIA

Occupation DRAUGHTSMAN (MECH.)

Passport No. ----- Country of issue of passport -----

NOTES

1. This voucher must be produced together with a valid passport to the Immigration Officer at the port of arrival in the United Kingdom. Failure to produce it may result in refusal of admission.
2. This voucher may be presented only by the person described therein.
3. This voucher cannot be used for entry to the United Kingdom after the date of expiry shown above, unless an extension has been granted. It does not entitle the holder to take work in Northern Ireland.

Signed on behalf of the Minister of Labour

E.D. 413 Date 7th February, 1963.

Image: Sample of a British ministry of labour voucher for commonwealth immigrant.

Illustration 4: Napier Drive, Tipton, UK
by Kulbir Colin Singh Dhillon

circa 1978

CHAPTER 3

Sorry no English

By 1976, my Mum and Dad had moved into their third home since arriving in England in 1968. To think that some people in England never move from their original home, and here we were already in our third house. This must have been seen as unusual for some of the stodgy people in our old neighbourhoods. The first home on Bloomfield road was a house our family shared with my Dad's elder and younger brother with their families. Next came Gospel Oak Rd, still in Tipton, and geographically closer to both Brickhouse Foundry, where all the three brothers worked. We occupied this house for five years, along with my Dad's younger brother's family, before moving to the entirely new and quite exclusive (well, for the Tipton area, at any rate) estate with approximately 40 homes. Napier Drive was the street upon which our corner house stood.

One of the first vivid memories I have of the house was the built-in fish tank under the stairs. See, in the 1970s, this was deemed terribly posh, and everyone in the extended family would talk about the fish tank because they either saw or heard about it!

We were the only *Sikh* or coloured family in the neighbourhood, something that was by design. One day after we had just moved in, the local children decided to provide us with a welcoming parade. They banged a discordant beat on toy drums and marched past our house on foot and on bicycles. They sang as they marched.

"*Pakis*, na, na, na…*Pakis,* na, na, na"

I remember being in the back garden and peering through a knothole in one of the fence panels. I could still recall their faces. Every detail is still vivid in my memory - siblings riding bikes with their younger siblings on the front handlebars or the rear of the bike. We didn't run inside to tell our parents. I think we just stood there, thinking about facing them at school once the holidays were over. I'm not sure we fully understood the meaning of what they were saying. Somehow, we could sense that the energy they were projecting was hostile and hateful.

We South Asians or East Indians didn't make it any easier to 'fit in' either. Let's take cooking for example. *Thorkah* is the name used for the essential base of ingredients used for most *Punjabi* dishes. It consists of onions, turmeric, garlic, ginger, cumin, salt, pepper, fried in *ghee* (purified butter; superfood). Yes, it sounds delicious, but its smell is potent! When *thorkah* or *Saag* (Spinach curry) was being prepared, holy crap, never mind the house, you would need to evacuate the whole bloody neighbourhood... hence the smelly *Paki* comments (most Indian people didn't change their clothes when going in and out of the house. All those potent fragrancies of curry are embedded into every strain of cotton, or linen or polyester you wear). Once out of your house and into the bland flavoured surroundings, wow did we stand out!

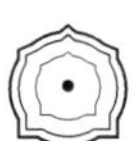

The English and the word *Paki*

I get it. Early Indian settlers in British Columbia, Canada, were referred to as *Hindus*. However, the vast majority of them were actually *Sikhs*. Why? Because it was the Imperial/Colonial British way of giving everything a different name. *Hindustanis* became *Hindus*. *Pakistanis* became *Pakis*. *Mumbai* became *Bombay*. There is power in renaming things to take ownership of them, but those four letters rolled off the tongue and attacked your inner peace. It never fails to get your blood boiling. Just hearing the word *Paki* generated anger within, and you can feel the serotonin being released through your body, even before the term was muttered by the cretin. It wasn't as simple as telling the local thug or bully, "Sorry, but I'm a *Sikh*" or "I'm an Indian." No, it didn't matter. The objective was simple; to make this word a venomous and degrading word which universally made the one it was used against feel humiliated and unwelcomed.

Though the welcoming committee had been somewhat hostile, the frosty reception melted away to reveal a more neutral base. Friendships were struck once everyone realized that the *Dhillon's* had actually moved into the neighbourhood for the exact same reasons as they did; better homes, like-minded families wanting their children to try and stay on the straight and narrow!

Not counting the adults, the neighbourhood consisted of the St. Johns (3), the Neil's (2), the Fowlers (1), and two sisters, Stacy and Karen. We were all pretty much the same age, give or take a few years, and we all had one thing in common. Unlike some of our friends at school, our parents got up every weekday morning and headed to work. Tipton was filled with those that lived off the social security system and comfortably drew the dole.

We would all converge to play outside my house. It was conveniently located at a T-junction in the sleepy neighbourhood. Most of us lived only a stone's throw away from each other. Living directly in front of my house was the "Stacy and Karen" show. These two sisters were, well, how do I say it..."friggin nuts". They were boisterous, and if they were not up to no good with someone on the street, they were certainly catfighting between themselves, hence the "Stacy and Karen Show".

I still remember one particular day during the summer of 1978. It was a glorious day and must have been a balmy 18 degrees Celsius. It was the kind of weather that the Brits call hot. The weather was warm enough to lose the shirts. I knew it was that warm because Stacy and Karen decided to cool down by having a water hose fight while running around their small inflatable paddling pool. My best friend was Mark Jackson, we were the same age. I was outgoing and somewhat loud, whereas Mark was the complete opposite (an introvert). He was the youngest of three with a significant age gap between him and his older sister, Michelle. Mark was spoiled with the latest toys and clothing. My parents didn't get the concept of toys. For them, it was a complete and utter waste of money, so I would typically play with Mark's toys. Mark had so many that the whole neighbourhood would play with them too!

On this particular summer holiday afternoon, I remember sitting on the edge of the curb with Mark. We were moving small pebbles that had become dislodged from the tarmac around in circular motions while we talked. Every now and then, we'd stop and examine a fingertip for dirt. When we could no longer make out the whorls that defined a fingerprint, we'd give the finger a quick wipe on a trouser leg.

We could get lost in the mundane, rather uneventful pace of daily life. Next, we would push pebbles around with one's finger one minute, or watch sycamore seeds fall, creating a spiral motion like a helicopter. It wasn't enough to just witness the natural process take place. Instead, we would try combining two sets of sycamore seeds together and then throwing them to the wind to advance their *airtime*. Mundane is what we felt when told to come back inside the house…outside was full of adventure.

We could hear shrieks, screams, and peals of laughter coming from across the road every now and then. The door to their garage was open, and we could see one or both sisters darting in and out of it. It was Stacy and Karen, and there was nothing they could do that would surprise us. We could hear their voices getting louder and shriller. What happened next was only the beginning of the Stacy & Karen show. They came running towards us, completely naked without a stitch of clothing on. They ran across the road, past our viewing point, and then circling back to their house. They were so completely caught up in their cat and dog chase scenario that I don't even think they saw us. They were free-spirited but a decade or so too late for the whole Woodstock event of the 1960s. I do believe we managed to get ourselves up and do our civic duty; we knocked on our friends' doors to tell them what was going on. The day ended as uneventfully as it began. The monotony was broken only for that single moment.

A few days passed, and the long days of summer meant that all the toys and games had been played with. Gradually, boredom was beginning to set in. This would have meant mischief for the average child but not for Stacy & Karen. I remember being summoned one day to Karen's house. She was the eldest of the two. She asked if I would play with her. After seeing poor Lee Fowler dragged home and spanked by his father for taking his clothes off and dancing in the small paddling pool at Karen's house, my answer was... NO! This wasn't received well because Karen was used to getting her way.

"OK," she said. "I'm gonna tell your Dad that you shagged me."

I knew quite well what shagged meant. It was a forbidden word that meant something wrong or off-colour.

"I don't care" was my response as I walked down her driveway without looking back.

"I'm not lying," she said. "You just wait until your Dad gets home."

"I don't care," I repeated in a slightly louder voice, as I began to cross the narrow street, making a beeline for my driveway.

My parents' schedules were like clockwork. At times, you could use their expected movements as a replacement for a clock. At 5 o'clock, my Dad would leave work. He would head for my Mum's workplace to pick her up and be home at precisely 5:14 pm.

On this particular day, our dinner time seemed no different than any other. Dad and Mum were discussing the usual topics with us. If any new observations or rules needed to be passed down to us, they were delivered at this time. My Dad sat directly in front of me, my brother to my left and my Mum to my right. I have always enjoyed small meal portions, and to be honest, I do not enjoy *Punjabi* food, especially homecooked. So, to help cater meals for my liking, potatoes would be added to pretty much every dish. I tend to shovel my food down fast as if every meal could possibly be my last. This usually meant that I was the first one to finish dinner. I often looked to get up and leave the table as soon as I was done before I would be given chores or told off for something I might have done. As I was about to get up, my Dad looked at me and said in *Punjabi*, "*Ohi, tu Karen nu Shag kith tha? Kabar dar*" which translated into English "Did you shag Karen? You better smarten up kid." This was all said with a frown, a deep furrow on his forehead, and a finger pointing towards me. I simply nodded, eyes wide open, catching the expression of my brother's face in the same stare.

"OK", I said.

What the hell just happened? Karen told my Dad that I shagged her, and my Dad just told me to stop shagging her and treat her like a sister. That wasn't a liberal father, telling his eight-year-old son to put his tool away…no sirree…what I heard was an unfortunate piece of slang not being fully comprehended. Luckily for me, my Dad didn't quite grasp what shagged meant, but my brother did. I'm not 100% sure, but when he walked past me after placing his dishes in the sink, he called me an idiot. This wasn't the first time he'd call me this, and it certainly wasn't going to be the last!

The following day, I went across the street and knocked on Karen's door. She opened it with a smirk on her face.

"I'm not your friend anymore," I said. I spun on my heels and walked away. I was very sure Karen was hurling some obscenities my way.

1978 was, in the large scheme of things, an infancy year for my parents' spiritual/religious quest/life change. It was quite typical for most *Sikh* men from the Doaba region of *Punjab* to arrive in England as turban-wearing *Sikhs* with unshorn hair. However, it wasn't long after they tried and 'assimilated' by removing their turbans and cutting their hair. My Dad arrived in England in

1968, but it wasn't until the early 1970s that he eventually cut his hair.

But assimilating to the "British" way of life wasn't something that sat well with him. He met a spiritual teacher in 1978 who changed everything for him and he stopped cutting his hair and reclaimed his crown; his turban.

These new changes and renewed commitments to faith meant changes for my brother and me as well. We had grown up cutting our hair. In 1978, we began to grow our hair and also started to wear turbans. Part of this religious shift for our household involved going back to religious/cultural basics.

The name of the *Sikh* place of worship is a *Gurdwara.* All *Gurdwara's* offer a free kitchen where a vegetarian meal is served to all those who enter. Culturally sitting on the floor; on rugs, in a cross-legged position was a normal practice representing equality for all. Sitting on chairs should not be seen as anything different - that is cultural in parts of the world too! We owned a lovely glass-topped kitchen table in our home, but to stay true to the cause, my Dad replaced our dining experience with a 3'x 3' table with 14" high legs mounted to it. Every dinnertime, we'd sit cross-legged on the floor and eat our dinner at this table, just like a proper English family. In contrast, the glass-topped, chrome-legged kitchen table stood in the background, staring down at us.

The Three Houses

Randomness:

CAPTAIN SINGH

Picture this; The *only Sikh boy in the early 1980s that wore a turban (I wore the turban while playing all sports other than swimming), lifting the coveted sports day trophy against his rival school. Movies have been based on weaker plots, I say!

I was twelve years old, and it was my final year at Primary School. One of my few talents growing up was being athletic. I was humbled in being a descendant of warriors, soldiers, and more recently, farmers. I understood how I could use my physicality and competitiveness to compete. I always felt inferior... second class, maybe? Perhaps, I needed to prove something because I was the brown turban-wearing boy who got called names by older children and their parents. Yet, I was intent on going toe-to-toe in the playground and earning my respect. That steely determination acted as an antidote when competing, and to be selected as the Captain of the school sports team was a high honour. What more does a young boy want as an accolade from both his peers and teachers?

As the Captain, I was expected to participate in critical events, including the 50-meter dash and the grand finale, the cricket ball toss.

To this day, I can still feel the adrenaline pumping through my body as I knew that I had clinched it. I wasn't the <u>Paki</u> but the Captain.

That day was a watershed moment for me. I understood that I would have to be better than my peers for me to be seen as equal.

Illustrations 5: Primary school athletics day trophy
by Kulbir Colin Singh Dhillon

---

*My elder brother, Rajesh had already left Primary School for High School, making me the only turban-wearing Sikh boy

Photo: Baba Ajit Singh Chaggar (Courtesy of Ajit Darbar)

CHAPTER 4
Man of God

What is God in the mind of an eight-year-old?
Who introduced it, and what does it mean to the child?

The concept of God goes back hundreds and thousands of years. If you have read *Yuval Noah Harari's* book, *Sapiens: A Brief History of Humankind*, then you will know that the concept of God might have been used to control people and as humans, we have been stargazing and paying homage to celestial beings.

The definition of God can be formless, ethereal, or human-like, and sometimes of the animal world. God has been described as a member of the male species more often than a Goddess *(Devi)* - both the embodiment of love and wrath; God apparently sees and hears everything...bla, bla, bla. You get the picture!

The concept of God can enter a child's mind from three channels; their home environment, schooling, and religious institutions. The visual imagery can depict a man with curly white hair perched upon a soft white cloud, or maybe a turban-wearing *Guru* who looks content sitting on his rock. Perhaps, it's a multilimbed individual loaded to the teeth with medieval weapons! The visual we imagine depends upon the faith being practiced in the house of that child, no? *Sikhs* depict their *Gurus*, some as elderly individuals, others as young men, but all fair-skinned and handsome. Hindu's have statues and paintings of their thirty-three million Gods. Let's not forget the retail store, God... Buddha; not sure I know of a house that doesn't have him sitting peacefully in some corner of their abode. I think it's safe to assume that the God of an eight-year-old could be hung up on the wall of his family room!

It was a slightly overcast day and we were on our way to meet a person my mum had described as a "Man of God". I guess it was the easiest way to explain to a child who a spiritually enlightened person is. I can recall some parts of the car journey to Coventry and some of my thoughts about this *Baba Ji* (an honorific title for a self-realized Master). *Baba Ajit Singh* was born on October 27th, 1919, in a village in *Punjab,* India. After retiring as a Currency Officer at the Reserve Bank of India, he began a mission to serve humanity through selfless service (*Seva*) and Meditation. He travelled the globe and planted seeds of love and compassion in the hearts and minds of all those that would listen.

Before this meeting, my only reference to God was images of the *Sikh Gurus*, *Krishna, Ram*, and Jesus. They all had one thing in common; halos around their heads! I began to wonder if this Man of God would also be decked out in a floating golden ring. Would he be too radiant for me to look at? Is he going to be even more critical than Santa; will I be on his naughty or nice list? The majority of our journey in the back of the Rover P6 was in silence, as I would often look out of the right-hand side window.

On our arrival at the *Gurdwara*, the congregation (*Sangat*) was bustling around the complex. I also noticed lots of other children, some around my age, what a relief! See, I was already planning on what to do for the rest of my time at the *Gurdwara*. I had the intention of meeting this *Baba Ji* and then sneak away and play! Initially, we were ushered into the main hall where we paid our respects to the eleventh *Guru* of the *Sikhs*, our scriptures known as the *Sri Guru Granth Sahib*. After which we were taken to another room.

I faintly recall all of us going into this room together (other family members from the Coventry area joined us). I remember feeling somewhat anxious because if this was a *Man of God*, he certainly could do miraculous things like reading one's mind. I think my brother may have even shed a few tears in the car because he was that nervous. However, what we saw was this little old man in his 60s, who was smartly dressed in a pair of trousers, a shirt, and a tie, wearing a colourful, printed turban (*dastar*), with his beard tied up. Upon seeing him, I was surprised. I guess I expected this god-like figure to be wearing a long white robe and turban, to be tall, and generally overpowering. I also remember feeling an instant connection to him. That day, the congregation must have included over 200 people, including approximately 20 children within my age group. Most of us, young chaps, sat along the corridor outside *Baba Ji's* room. A senior member of the congregation outlined the rules of engagement, which included standing when *Baba Ji* walks by and sitting only when he re-entered his room. This was seen as a sign of respect. Every time he walked by, we all stood up and only sat down when he returned to his room; over a period of four hours. I'm sure that only occurred twice, but I swear it felt like several times. Being new to the congregation and this whole environment meant we stayed put, otherwise there would have been no chance that you'd catch me sitting down like a good little boy.

Baba Ji glanced over, making eye contact with me a few times. I vividly remember feeling in awe of him. Immediately, I thought that this individual was someone special, someone, who had people prostrating. But I assumed my feelings were felt by everyone else, and I understood his glance to be the same for everyone too. I believe the reason we had all gathered was that *Baba Ji* was about to leave the United Kingdom and head back to India. Most of the congregation seemed to be local to the City of Coventry. We were the newcomers, but it all seemed reasonable like you would feel at home or with family and friends.

When *Baba Ji* was finally about to depart, the people encircled him; about fifty people all standing in broken concentric circles. He was a short man, approximately five feet three inches. As *Baba Ji* stood in the centre of the hall with all his followers

clasping their hands and smiling with wide-eyed expressions, he said his farewell. He asked all to live by the tenets given to us by the *Sikh Gurus*. Then he said,
"Today, somebody here has given me so much love."
(I didn't hear this, I was told after the event).

I was standing on the outer circle with some of my new-found friends, partially paying attention to what was being said and feeling glad that we would be going home soon. Let's face it, what 8-year-old wants to be held within one particular environment for more than thirty minutes!

As *Baba Ji* was making his statement, he began walking towards me. The sea of people began to part (it was like the story of Moses walking through the Red Sea…not really, that's just too overdramatic). He stood about four feet away from me and signalled me to approach him. I do remember doing the 'film-like-thing' and looking around and asking,
"Me?"

He nodded. As I approached, he picked me up and said,
"This child today has shown me the most love."

I still remember looking for my parents. I didn't understand a lot, but I did recognize that the Man of God whom we had travelled from Tipton to see had selected me. To be honest, I did feel a connection. I didn't know how to explain it or evaluate it. I thought the feelings rushing through me were normal and that everyone was feeling them as well. Looking back on that event, I recall feeling a deep relationship with other beings present there too; I felt really connected. At some level, blood relationships are not necessarily the strongest of connections in ones emotional and physical being. The bond through love is far more superior. This man showered me with love. Until this moment, I understood love to be shared with your parents, siblings, and close family. A stranger had just professed a universal love, a love of the purest kind, not just for me, but the *REAL* me… (that who dwells within). This precise event, I feel changed my outlook on life.

Baba Ji would go on to be a large part of both my life and my family's. For years, as I grew older I would spend several days and nights working selflessly on building projects at the *Gurdwara* (which used to be an old Church built in the early 1900s). I assisted the Electrician, Plumbers, and Bricklayers. When the new boundary wall of the *Gurdwara* was to be completed, the bricklayer was willing to work till the early hours of the morning. I was there to pass the bricks and clean the mortar. Don't get me wrong, I was also at the forefront of messing around and getting up to no good. Still, the deep internal connection to *Baba Ji* and the *Sikh* way of life was beginning to blossom from within.

Baba Ji was a simple man. His message, like most true godmen/women, was love. He kept it simple for the most part, asking the congregation to focus on the tenants of the *Sikh* faith;

1. ***Kirt Karna*** - *Earn an honest living*
2. ***Vand ke Chhakna*** - *Share with others*
3. ***Naam Japna*** - *Meditate (connecting with yourself and the cosmic energy)*

Looking back at that initial meeting, I try to dissect the *look* that *Baba Ji* gave me. One can express oneself beyond mere words, facial and bodily expressions. The "look" (merciful grace) in the East is also described as *Nadar*, and something spiritual that occurs between a teacher/guru and the student/disciple. What was it that attracted *Baba Ji* to me? I didn't speak a word; my look would have been filled with curiosity rather than an indescribable glance of the disciple paying homage to his *Guru*. Still, I did feel in awe of him. I looked up and saw a Man of God in the presence of my family and a congregation of believers.

As I grew from a child into a young man, *Baba Ji* was always present at the forefront, of our lives. The months he spent in the United Kingdom added both excitement and spiritual stimulation for some of the congregation. For others, it was an opportunity to play politics! One would think that this gentle godly being was charismatic and an elite *card-carrying* member of the cosmic-being institution. His *nadar* forty-two years ago might well have changed my life's path... my way of living, and my outlook on life's journey.

"He alone appreciates the value of Your love,
upon whom You shower Your grace, O Lord"

"prem kee saar soiee jaanai jis no nadhar tumaaree jeeau"

- Sri Guru Granth Sahib (page 1016)

Randomness:

INFLUENTIAL FIGURES (NOT IN ANY PARTICULAR ORDER):

We all have them, no? People that have helped to shape the individuals we are today, but sometimes these individuals might have managed to influence us even without them knowing. Historical figures that one reads about can be highly influential. You read a sanitized version of their lives and achievements through the lens of a historian/biographer, but so what...it motivated you, right?

My list of influential people is compiled of characters from a diverse spectrum of backgrounds; some might be musicians, parents, spouses, political figures, and spiritual beings. One thing they all have in common is the strength of character. Make your own list.

Guru Nanak – Nelson Mandela – J.R.R. Tolkien – John Lennon – Malcolm X – Shaheed Bhagat Singh – Satinder Dhillon - Ralph Gilles - Guru Teg Bahadur - Martin Luther King Jr. – Rashpal Singh Dhillon – Baba Ajit Singh – Jessie Owens - Gautama Buddha - Leonardo da Vinci – Bhai Kanhayia - Guru Gobind Singh – Muhammad Ali – Rajesh Dhillon - Gurbaksh Kaur Dhillon - Kenny Dalglish – Elvis - Flavio Volpe – Mr. Richardson - Mr. Bates – Bruce Lee - Maharani Jind Kaur - Michael “Pinball” Clemons

---

Illustration 6: Sir King Kenny. #YNWA
by Kulbir Colin Singh Dhillon

KIN

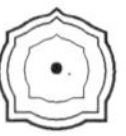

CHAPTER 5a
White Power

Being the only two turban-wearing boys in a high school of 1600 students in the early 1980s was not easy, especially when being a skinhead was quite fashionable in those dark days. Skinheads and the larger white nationalist movement flourished at a time of national socio-economic depression, driven by a lack of employment and job stability. The target of their rage was visible minorities who, in their eyes, had deprived them of their god-given right to work and wealth. In their skewed world view, we were taking opportunities that should have been rightfully theirs. These Skinheads thudded around in their industrial boots, looking for a chance to clobber someone, and we were easy targets, especially with those colourful turbans our father would tie on us.

England has always been an island of diversity, more than most people know or will admit to. There have been people of colour living in England since Roman times. The vast Roman empire spanned across most of present-day Europe and parts of North Africa. People of the Empire belonged to many races and creeds. African Legionnaires served in the province of Britannia around the 5th Century AD. Some chose to settle there and called Britain home. With the English empire stretching from East to West, the influx and settlement of people of colour could only be expected. In 1856, the first *Sikh* arrived in England. His Royal Highness, *Maharajah Duleep Singh*, was the exiled monarch of the Sikh Kingdom. His son, Prince Victor Albert *Jay Duleep Singh* became the first of Sikh origin to be born in England (Coincidentally, he was the first of Sikh origin to arrive in Canada). For more information on Prince Victor, please watch my documentary movie, The Lion That Lost His Roar, at: *www.victorduleepsingh.com*

Truth be told, bigotry is well within the reach of most of us, but it takes a special kind of a nut job to make racism a life-long career. To pass judgement on others that have a different skin colour to yours or different clothing, even sometimes when you know an individual personally, is cruel. To blame visible minorities for the lack of economic growth of one's town, city, region or country, is entirely absurd, narrow-minded, and the furthest thing from the truth, yet, skinheads and their numbers were on the rise.

British comedy and dramas are appreciated the world over. TV shows from the UK in the 1970s and 80s might have unknowingly provided fodder for some characters we minorities would meet in society. How many times did I have to hear about being a *paka wala* (It Ain't Half Hot Mum - 1974), being called *Ranjit* (Mind Your Language - 1977), or *Gunga Din* (1890 Poem by Rudyard Kipling and the 1930's movie starring Cary Grant). Though by far the most common one at school had to be,

"Hey, I'm Gripper" (Grange Hill, Season 6 - 1983). Yes, I guess it was good to see people that supposedly looked like me on the television, but it really didn't help on a micro-level.

What is a Skinhead?

Like with any community that seeks to group together with like-minded people, their physical appearance is their signature. It is used to identify them with one another and the community at large. Their one commonality was their lack of hair. They either sported a fully shaved head or a very low-grade trim. Their clothing consisted of tight blue denim jeans rolled up to just above the ankle, over on the shin of the leg with Doc Marten boots, preferably in oxblood colour. Their signature mark was the red laces on their boots — a Ben Sherman shirt or Fred Perry half-sleeved collared shirt with a green or black bomber jacket. The uniform was unisex to an extent. There was something about these groups of wankers that made you feel overwhelmed and to be honest, shit scared! If several regular looking thugs had infiltrated their ranks and they were fast approaching, the fact that they were not all skinheads made them less daunting.

In an economically depressed town like Tipton, the social security safety net supported hundreds, if not thousands of its residents. Out of this depression, some lower social strata were being created. Immigrants coming to Tipton to work at the depleting factories and foundries did not help. It was easy to demonize immigrants with the rhetoric of 'those *Pakis* have come to our country and are taking our jobs' all the while these people are living off the state. It's needless to say, while their parents lived off welfare, the children were being recruited into the white nationalist movement. So, when you are one of two people attending high school wearing a turban, life will be challenging, to say the least.

Blessed are the uniform gods because without them, school would have been that much more daunting. Our school uniform consisted of a black blazer with a white shirt and a grey, blue, or burgundy jumper along with a tie high-lighting our school colours. All the students were expected to come dressed in uniform every day. Any student found guilty of not following the regulation would be sent home.

Though having a 'skinned head' was the mark of these morons, their colours, and their marks were safely covered under the uniform that we all had to wear. It's incredibly challenging to look threatening in a burgundy jumper worn over a shirt and tie. Most teachers were not fond of those 'suspect' skinheads. What was acceptable and unacceptable was all determined by teachers. And why not, might I add! When you spend a quarter of your day in their presence being nurtured, educated, and disciplined, it only makes sense (something which seems to be lost on educational authorities today). Those students who showed signs of their affiliation with skinhead culture were made to feel that

---

*Yes, I can be considered as broadly stereotyping and generalizing slightly however these statements are based upon my personal experiences.

any outward signs of racism were unacceptable, nor would they be tolerated.

Tipton was scattered with skinheads and littered with racists. You only had to go off the beaten paths of society, around the canals and industrial parks, and behold, a small group would appear like ground worms after a Spring shower. I grew up looking hundreds-of-meters ahead in the direction I was going, either on foot or on my bike. If one or a group were spotted, I would be left with only a few options; turn around and run in the direction I was coming from, cross the street, and hope that they had already met their intake of *Paki*-bashing or hurling racial slurs, or simply continue walking, staying on course IF surrounded by friends, preferably with my white friends! I found myself taking option one for the most part and live to tell my story.

Dad had a noticeable scar on his left forearm, snaking from the soft inner part of his arm, towards the back of his hand, for as long as I could remember. Though I had noticed it many-a-time, it wasn't until I was in my late teens that I asked how he came about getting such a disfigurement.

Dad shared the following... "It was 1977, and your mum used to catch the bus to work and back. On the morning bus commute, on a jam-packed double-decker bus, a young white man would call your mum names, like "fucking *Paki*", every day. She only shared this with me after he wouldn't stop with the racially motivated foul language, for over a week. I told ya, mum, to catch the bus, as usual, the next day, but at her stop, when she and the bloke got off the bus, I asked her to point him out and I would take care of the rest".

"I stood about six meters away from the bus stop, as hundreds of people bustled past me to work. It was around 7:20 am. As your mum stepped off the bus, she pointed him out. I quickly walked towards him and shouted, OI, YOU BASTARD, and punched him in the face and we grappled on the bloody ground. As we both got up, he began to run, and I chased him down, he began to fall against a wall, as he fell, he grabbed onto a broken wooden pallet and swung the object, with nails protruding, at me. One of the nails hit my forearm and gave me this scar. He got up and ran. I think he got the message. As I dusted off the dirt, I looked around at all those people that had stopped to watch the fight... they all carried on their way to work. Your mum never had an issue again with that bastard!"

Post-Brexit: 2020

Forty years later, multiple Governments and their policies have all left their mark on British law and its society. Racist policies and a flat out restriction to people originating from *developing* nations should have allowed England and its residents to do a root-cause analysis of their race issues. Decades have passed for British society to finally come to terms with people of colour that are born in Britain are, in fact, British!

"I'm not racist, but..."

The vote to leave the European Union (EU) was not based solely on the country's financial burden or economic state; instead, the people of Britain voted to stop the immigration from Europe, more specifically, Poland. Britain's woke up to the shocking news that they had exited the EU. The DNA of the majority chose to stem the flow of the latest foreigners. Why? Because they were taking jobs away? Changing the British culture? The United Kingdom has more than 800,000 Polish nationals, one of the most significant ethnic minorities in the country. The Polish language is the second-most spoken language in England. Though they may not stand out like the Indian, Jamaican and Pakistani immigrants, you can hear their accents and voices all over the United Kingdom. That's the problem. They have taken our jobs and taking advantage of our social welfare programs. They have to be stopped…

For over the past five years, hate crimes in the United Kingdom have doubled. Nationalism is on the rise, not only because of British politicians and their politics but also because of 'dog whistlers' running nations like the United States and India. Ambivalent attitudes in British society have always allowed racism to fester. The class societies, like the United Kingdom and India, help to divide its people. The working-class or those less fortunate (materialistically) feel as though they can never escape from this hole. It's a life sentence with little or no chance for parole.

It's time for the United Kingdom and other nations to change their policies. Nothing short of this will actually work. Maybe the 5th Industrial Revolution will assist. Perhaps, cognitive technology implants, like *Neurolinks* can help to eradicate those deep-lying thoughts and feelings of hatred! It's a top-down approach, but it requires the people to elect leaders of nations that aim to uplift society and its members. For policymakers to weed out legislation and regulations that might be influencing the White Power types.

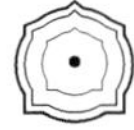

The Three Houses

Randomness:

THE VENICE OF ENGLAND.

In 1712, the world's first successful steam pumping engine was erected at the Coneygree Coalworks by Thomas Newcomen and James Watt. Tipton was the beating heart of the Black Country. The steam engine heralded in the era of the Industrial revolution. Along with steam power came the inlaying of canals. Tipton, the Venice of the Midlands, is dissected with hundreds of waterways. These canals served the most essential service in the era of the Industrial Revolution. The transportation of both raw and finished goods, long canal barges being dragged by horsepower.

This spaghetti bowl of waterways was a place of intrigue and adventure for any delinquent teenagers. Sometimes when we walked to school, we would take a shortcut through large canal junctions. Some of us, usually Jason, Mark, and I would hoist ourselves up onto the handrail portion of the bridge. We would spread our arms and walk across the bridge, toe to heel, like tightrope walkers. Life was about taking risks.

Illustration 7: Tipton Canal by Rajesh Singh Dhillon (1986)

Illustration 8: Graffiti - National Front
by Kulbir Colin Singh Dhillon

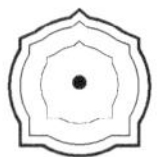

CHAPTER 5b
Daily Dose of Racism

When I look back at my early childhood, I realize that I had to accept the racism in order to make things easier for myself. At home, my parents sympathized with us, but they didn't really understand our daily dilemmas.

Though they both worked in predominantly white workplaces, where they faced a fair share of racial discrimination, they were both adults when they arrived in the United Kingdom. For the most part, they had already developed their sense of identity as *Sikhs* in India. Moving to the United Kingdom was their choice. In comparison, being born in Britain, being a visible minority, being a turban-wearing *Sikh*, these were NOT my choices. When you choose to take a journey, you accept the challenges thrown in your path and try to overcome them. However, if by uncontrollable circumstances, you are forced on a journey you had no say over, it becomes difficult to accept and overcome those same challenges.

---

*Graffiti: The National Front was a far-right political party (fascist or neo-fascist ideology) founded in Britain, in the 1960s. The National Front (party) 'NF' acronym was usually sprayed on building surfaces by Skinheads and other racists, symbolizing the right-wing views, and acting as a statement to new and old immigrants, to be aware.

Illustration 9: Alexandra High School Annex, Birch Street, Tipton. UK
by Kulbir Colin Singh Dhillon

Alexander High School was annexed into two institutes; the first, second, and, third year students spent most of the week at the 'lower-end', a Victorian red brick building on Birch Street in Tipton. Geographically, it was about a thirty-five-minute walk from my house. The main school campus was on Alexandra Road, which was less than a ten-minute walk from home.

I was 13 and Yossa was nearly 16. On paper, 13 and 16 don't seem too far apart…it's only a mere three years. In high school though, a three-year age gap can feel like decades apart, in terms of both physical and mental growth, street smartz, seniority, and self-confidence.

My first encounter with Yossa happened in my first year of high school, right after finishing History class. My History teacher was also my Physical Education (P.E.) teacher. The relevance of having him as my P.E teacher will be shared later in the story. When the class finished, I was asked to take some textbooks to the History department storage room. This meant that I had to walk across a small section of the schoolyard to get there. It was the end of the first period after lunch, and nobody was walking around the school, the yard was also deserted. As I walked across the grounds, carrying the heavy load of textbooks, I noticed a group of guys by the school gates, which were about 10 meters from where I was. I immediately recognized Yossa and another pupil who was in the same year as my brother. Yossa was a pretty boy, standing around 5' 7", weighing about 140 lbs. He was dark-haired and wasn't dressed in his uniform, but rather his casual clothing. He had built a reputation for himself as a scrapper. I never knew if this was due to a single brawl or multiple scraps, but the word-of-mouth was such that even first year students like us had already heard of the legend of Yossa. Though he didn't dress in the skinhead garb, there was no doubt that he was definitely the leader of a band of racists. Yossa called and his gang answered, and they looked to him for direction.

It was a typical English autumn day; damp and overcast. The asphalt seemed to glisten, which meant that the rain had come and gone at some point in the past few hours. I glanced at the group but continued to walk towards the storage room with my head down. Then all of a sudden it came...

"*Paki*!"

The word was tossed in my direction, and like a pack of hyenas, they began to cackle and jog towards me. Now, I was using my peripheral vision, walking forward, but slightly to the left, which was in the opposite direction to the gang. I began to walk faster, but it only took them a few seconds before I was surrounded.

"Little *Paki*" and "You fuckin' *Paki*" was being spat at me as I now stood cornered against a brick wall and the side of a porto-cabin classroom.

I was still holding the pile of textbooks. The content on the pages of these books talked about the brave British men and women who stood up to the tyranny and oppression of the Nazi war machine away from home. Ironically, their children and grandchildren promoted racial division and maltreatment on home soil. My senses were on full alert. Instantly, somebody stepped on my foot, another pushed me and then I felt a punch to the side of my body.

"Hey, stop, or I'll tell my teacher!", I said. It was all I had in my verbal arsenal. Words felt trapped in my throat, unable to come out in defence.

"Yeah…try it, you little *Paki* bastard", Yossa said, as he punched me on the side of my neck. I began to move my head side-to-side, in short split seconds, trying to make sure that he doesn't knock off my turban; it was the one thing I never wanted to see happen. I had been wearing a turban to school since I was eight years old. I had been well trained by my parents in knowing that no matter what happened to me, my turban (crown) was never to fall, unlike Richard III's at the Battle of Bosworth Field (August 22nd, 1485).

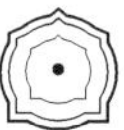

Randomness:

HEAVY IS THE HEAD THAT WEARS THE...
TURBAN, DASTAAR, PAGRI, PAGG OR CROWN

The names associated with the turban worn by Sikhs. It is also an article of faith that represents honour, self-respect, courage, spirituality, and piety. The turban represented nobility and royalty under the Mughal rulers of India. It is also a practical way of keeping the unshorn hair of a Sikh in place, as well as acting as a protection from sunstroke and in time of war.

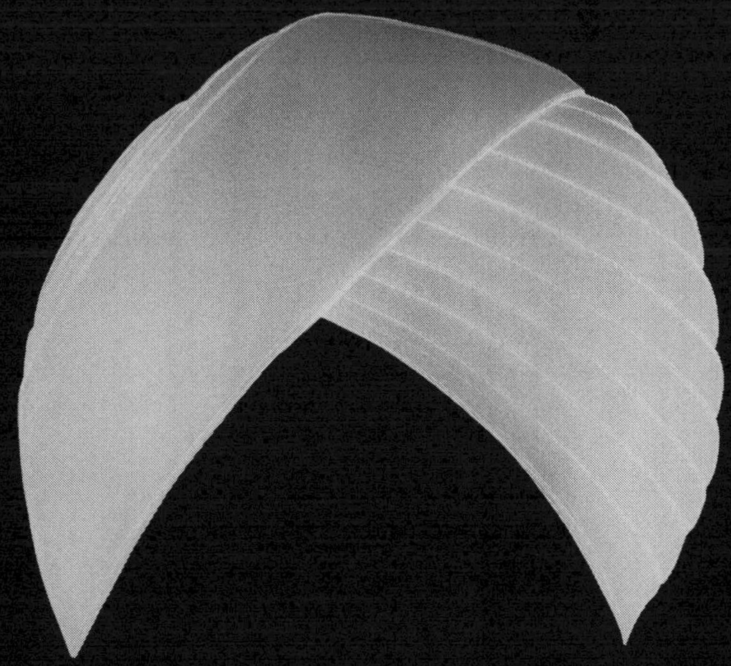

Illustration 10: My Turban
by Kulbir Colin Singh Dhillon (2020)

I think the frenzy and possibly my cries for help must have caught the attention of my History teacher, Mr. Starkey. He came up to the window and banged his clenched fists against the glass panels, creating a thumping noise that caught Yossa and his riffraff's attention. I looked up to see the strong bearded face of Mr. Starkey shouting at the gang. Immediately, they turned around to look at him. Some of them hurled obscenities at him, but the fact is that they had forgotten about me for a split second. Mr. Starkey peeled himself off the glass and moved away out of sight. Everyone knew what that meant, he wasn't going back to continue with the class, he was heading straight for the outside door (Something our PE Teachers seemed to be up for, was a good old scrap. Annually, our school was visited by Willingsworth High School...for a fight. Students would be kept indoors until the Willingsworth lot had been dispersed, but only after the PE teachers went out and smacked a few of them about). Now a few of these characters were still in school; the others had quit school or had been expelled. Those that still had relations to the school began to head for the school gate. Mr. Starkey would have come out in a position that would have blocked their access point. The rest followed, understanding the possible checkmate position that they were about to be put in.

Though the whole bullying incident only lasted a few seconds, it felt like minutes. I was scared! Prior to this encounter, I had never been surrounded by several individuals that didn't know me, which I had not said or done anything to, yet wanted to attack and humiliate me. To this day, it only takes me a few seconds, at any given moment, to relive that ordeal. I remember standing there, still holding the full stack of textbooks, probably feeling proud that I'd managed to keep them from tumbling onto the wet hard ground. I watched as the gang moved towards the gate and as Mr. Starkey appeared and ran down the four steps towards them. A few colourful words were hurled Mr, Starkey's way as they began to run through the gate and beeline it. Mr. Starkey approached me and asked if I was okay. I replied that I was, and made him know that I managed to keep the textbooks from dropping. He smiled and I guess he would have wanted to just pat the top of my head and ruffle my hair, but I had a turban on! Instead, he patted me on my right shoulder. I carried the books to the storage room while the teacher stood on guard in-between the two zones, and we walked back to the classroom together. I shared my ordeal with my friends, however, sympathy was not something 13-year-old boys gave out in spades. If anything, I probably got mocked for being attacked!

---

*My Turban Fact: Throughout these ordeals, protecting my turban was always paramount. I can proudly say that nobody ever knocked off my turban whilst making eye contact with me. Yes, sneaking up from behind, surrounded by a large crowd in the corridors, it occurred a few times...but NEVER face to face.

Over the next few weeks, I had several encounters with Yossa and his gang. They didn't live nearby and most of them were not even attending school anymore, but they still made their presence known. My next run-in with this group was on the way home on my normal route, but I was fortunate to see them all from over 400 meters and that gave me time to circle back and take another route. My next encounter occurred along the canal, the waterways of our Venice of England. I had decided to take a different route home. The canal route was unique in that from a certain point you only had one entry/exit point after walking for over 15 minutes. As I approached the wire fence with a large hole in its structure, I noticed a skinhead approaching. I stopped and the two friends I was walking with also stood dead in their tracks.

A second skinhead appeared and then Yossa. They hadn't seen me yet, but it was inevitable that they would. All they had to do was slightly turn to their right as we were only about 10 meters away from where they stood. I told my friends to run just as I started to run the fourteen or so minutes in the opposite direction, something I didn't think I'd be able to do.

I was dressed in full school uniform, blazer and all. Backpacks were not our thing in England, we normally carried sports bags that are usually hung diagonally across our chests. I grabbed the short handles to give me less momentum from the contents of my bag as I started to run.

The next thing I heard was, "Oi, *Paki*".

I told my friends to stop running as Yossa and his riffraff were after me and not my white friends. I continued, but I kept looking over my shoulder. A year prior, I was the captain of my school's athletic team, and at some point, we had challenged a local school and brought home the cup. I had always been a bit of a jock, someone that enjoyed physical activities, but I was also asthmatic, which prevented me from running long distances, anything over 600 meters. I stopped in my tracks.

It only took them a few seconds to catch up with me. The usual "You fucking *Paki*", "*Raghead*" salutations began to be hurled at me. They circled me…well, half-circled me, while I backed up towards the canal.

"I haven't done anything to you." That was the only thing I could remember saying to them. What does a bully get out of terrorizing an individual, especially one that was a lot younger than they are?

They moved closer. I was being pushed rather than punched this time and I took my bag off knowing what was about to happen.

Every course at school required a notebook and every book had to be covered. Yes, at the beginning of the school year, students would usually find different materials, mostly paper coverings to use as a cover for their notebooks. Mine were neatly covered with wallpaper that had been leftover from decorating the bedroom and hallway at home. I made sure not to use the red velvet wallpaper from our living room, as that would have given my friends free fodder at my expense. At this point, I stood less than two feet from the edge of the canal. The pushing continued until finally, as I was pushed closer to the edge, I turned around wanting to make sure I was in control of two things; the way I fell into the canal and also to make sure my turban was not going to get wet if I ended up being pushed more horizontally than vertically.

As I broke the surface of the water, expecting to be struggling to stay afloat, I found that the level of water was at my chest level. The floor of the canal was slightly uneven, but I managed to steady myself. Then I stood, about 2 meters from the edge, looking at Yossa and his gang of wankers. They laughed, spat at me, and hurled some more raghead slurs, and all the time my school bag just sat there unharmed. I consciously made sure that I didn't stare at my bag to avoid them noticing it. The thought of having to wrap a new set of books and explaining to my teachers why they had become wet and soggy in the first place was running through my head like coding on a computer screen.

I simply waited, feeling a sense of security in the cold waters of the canal. The pressure of the body of water around me was holding me, comforting me. The initial shock was gone, now I knew the idiots would not want to come after me again. After all, they have achieved what they wanted to do… "threw a fucking *Paki* into a canal". It might have been a first for them, something to brag about, I guess!

As they got bored of seeing me in the canal, something that unfolded in seconds rather than minutes, they began walking away in the opposite direction towards my way home. I watched until they were at least 30 meters away before slowly making my way up to the edge of the canal, being careful of the house bricks and other debris at the bottom of the canal. I pulled myself up and onto the edge of the canal and I stood up. I grabbed my school bag and walked briskly towards the hole in the wire fence. After passing through the hole and looking back over my shoulder a number of times, I began to remove the layers of my drenched clothing. I still had over twenty minutes and some uncharted territory to walk through. The surrounding areas to our estate were littered with council estates, known breeding grounds for racists and their strong xenophobic beliefs, which were passed down to their children. These minefields had to be passed before I could safely get home.

I did get some looks because when somebody is drenched and soaked, you tend to walk a wee bit differently, leaving wet footmarks as a trail. With my limbs held out from my body and with every step loudly squelching, I resembled a 'B' Movie Egyptian Mummy more than anything else.

I got home, removed my clothing, being careful not wet the carpet in the house, and only had my underwear on. Grasping my clothes close to my chest, I ran upstairs to the washroom. I dumped my clothes inside the bathtub and prepared to wash them. I don't think I bathed or showered. Why did I wash my clothes? Because I didn't want my parents to know about the bullying I was going through. I am a *Sikh*; my clan and my people were warriors, a Martial race; my 10th Guru's children happily sacrificed their lives for their beliefs and faith. The measly bullying was not a big enough deal. In fact, I was embarrassed that I didn't fight back or at least try to defend myself against this gang of racists. I guess I knew what would have occurred if I fought back. Black eyes, possible broken appendages, and maybe the possibility of being stabbed by one of the glue-sniffing, high as a kite, gang members.

The following day, I went to school as normal. I walked to school with my friends and filled them in on my ordeal, probably slightly exaggerating the story and making it sound even more dramatic, but the simple fact was it was another day for a new adventure.

A few weeks later, I had the final encounter of the year with Yossa and the skinheads while I was walking home from school, along my regular street route. As I came close to halfway, I noticed Yossa. He instantly began to run towards me with five or six other skinheads. Again, I broke away from my friends and I knew I was only a few hundred yards from my auntie's shop (The *Bains*'). I crossed the street and ran, down someone's garden path, furiously checking over my shoulder. I was panting as I began to knock at the door. They came up to the edge of the property line and one of them said "You don't live there". I said, "My auntie does", even though it was not my aunty's house and began knocking on the door with my right hand…something kept them at bay, as they didn't advance. They stood there and hurled a few warm "*Paki*" greetings my way and tried to spit on me from about 4 meters away. Then, they moved away. I waited for about 30 seconds, thinking about the distance to my auntie's shop and as soon as I could, I ran. They immediately turned around and began to chase me. Now it was a race in which I had less than 200 meters to run. This was something I was good at and the fact that I felt like I was running for my dear life also put extra wind behind my sails. They gave me a chase, closing the gap as I got close to my auntie's shop. I started to shout, and my uncle appeared. My uncle *Bains'* was over six feet tall and his presence was enough, not to mention his verbal onslaught of "Oi, Fuck off you bastards". I nestled behind him and then straight into the shop.

Though I had managed to survive a beating by the skinheads, I also managed to make the situation larger. Now, my uncle was involved, and he would take me home. When my parents were informed about the situation, I opened up and told them that the bullying had been going on for quite some time. My Dad talked about involving the police, but both my brother and I told him it would be of no use as these delinquents were not going to change. The society and all of its rules were there to be broken, not followed. It was decided that I become more vigilant and maybe notify the Headmaster about the situation with the thought of getting a teacher's escort when leaving the classroom in the school hallways, or heading for the school gates. However, I chose to do nothing. As much as it was horrifying when the chase would occur, it somehow felt normal and something I could, might I say, live with. See, you would get a similar type of response from your teachers when you informed them that an individual used a racial slur against you. Most would not tolerate it and swift action would be taken, though the punishment compared to today's hypersensitivity, would usually mean detention and/or a visit to the deputy or headmaster's office. Some would simply say, "Pack it in or else?" Teachers brushing off racist slurs with a mild scolding meant you had to put your head down and just get on with it.

But then, it suddenly stopped, just like an electrical panel switch had slammed down and turned the power off. One day, I was being bullied and then, like taking a needle off a record, there was silence. It just stopped don't get me wrong, the odd "*paki*" would still be hurled in my direction, but I didn't see any member of the gang until the spring of 1988.

Tipton was flanked by two towns of particular interest; if you wanted to go shopping, you would need to go to West Bromwich, the birthplace of none other than Robert Plant, the lead singer of Led Zeppelin. The other was Dudley, the home of English comedian, Sir Lenny Henry. You needed to visit either one for your basic clothing apparel needs. If you wanted a particular brand/label, then you'd need to go to the City of Birmingham. On this occasion, I was coming back from West Bromwich with a few friends and we were set to get off at Dudley Port, right outside the post office. As we entered the double-decker bus, we headed straight upstairs to find a seat. Sitting on the back row was Yossa with two others. Now things had changed slightly since 1983. I had always been tall for my age, well at least in high school, and I was never a skinny, scrawny kid. I enjoyed physical activities and to be honest, I lived in the saddle of a bike for most of my childhood life. I was now 17 approaching 18. I graduated high school as being supposedly the **Cock* of the school because; (i) my classmates were deemed to be the toughest chaps in our year and therefore by default, I must have been tough too, and (ii) a so-called fight with a local scrapper, who was older than me, decided he didn't want to fight me due to my physical size. These situations elevated my *cock* status.

Yossa saw me as I glanced at him and acknowledged to myself that it was in fact him. Now, the twenty or so minute journey was shadowed with the fact that this bastard was sitting on the back row of the same bus. I was becoming agitated and the thoughts/ nightmares of that period of my life came gushing into my consciousness. Though I carried on a normal conversation with my friends, I was preoccupied with the past. As our stop was approaching, we got up to walk down the stairs. I was the last one of the three of us. Behind me came Yossa…as we spiralled

---

*Violence was an important part of the educational experience of many British children during the nineteenth and twentieth centuries. It principally took the form of playground fights, in which children competed in displays of physical prowess to win the accolade "cock of the school," the term attached to the best fighter. (The Cock of the School: A Cultural History of Playground Violence in Britain, 1880–1940 by Jacob Middleton)

down the staircase, just about 3 steps from the bottom. He placed a hand on my left shoulder and said, "No hard feelings, *Dhill*".

He was never a gigantic physical specimen; instead, he was below average height. That 'small man syndrome' was obviously at play. He was charismatic, I guess an evil little shit, someone who used his mental strength and verbal dexterity to overcome any physical fight situations, plus he probably had many fights. He was an experienced hand at it.

I turned around and said, "Fuck you, Yossa" and turned back, stepping now onto the second and then the last step. "Wow, easy now, *raghead*", he replied. The inner Kraken; that mythological monster that could cause destruction beyond words. I put my head down and held the pole with my right hand just before the exit step off the bus. The bus stop was right outside a pub. If I recall, it had a façade of stones rather than bricks and it was barely 3 meters from the edge of the road. As we were disembarking, the picture of what was about to happen played out in my head, similar to a Quentin Tarrantino movie, minus the squirting blood and musical score. I stepped down to exit the bus, and just as I exited, I quickly turned around and grabbed Yossa by the back collar of his jacket and began to move quickly. I went straight towards the pub wall with Yossa's head positioned like a medieval battering ram. As he made contact with the stone wall and then fell back, I stood ready for the next scene to play out.

The times they had cornered me, pushed and kicked me, spat at me and howled racial slurs in my direction came flooding in like a *tsunami.* At no point had any one of them really given me a savage beating, but it didn't matter. For five years, I carried those feelings and even carried myself in a manner where I would not be noticed by the wrong crowd. My friends who knew me would comment on the fact that I would always walk through the corridors with my head down and my left foot would be facing inwards on my instep. Basically, I was reducing my physical presence, trying not to make eye contact because you never knew what would kick off…

As he lay on his back, clutching his head, I did what I'd always stopped my friends at school from doing in a fight situation. I stomped on his face and head. Tears were rolling down my face. I began shouting "Fuck you, Yossa" as I repeatedly pummeled him. I could hear distant shouting, but I was so lost that I had no idea who it was or why they were shouting. Yossa's two friends stood there watching as I humbled their friend. A small crowd of people was beginning to gather. It was the bus driver shouting and then slowly I became aware of my surroundings. My friends came over and carted me away from doing the *Shiva* dance of destruction on his head. I was overcome with anger and what must have been years of pent-up frustration, and anxiety was unleashed in a matter of seconds. I wiped away the tears from my cheeks and when asked by friends if I was okay, I told them that I was. I then hurriedly made my way home on my own, looking over my shoulder, still wondering if a gang of skinheads would ambush me. I was almost disappointed when none did. To avenge myself and to lay those ghosts to rest internally was, truth be told...satisfying.

Today, I smile more than I frown. I stay to help my fellow human beings rather than choosing the easier option of walking away. Why? Contentment, maybe. I am not angry at society although sometimes I feel I have every right to be. I have earned the right to walk around proudly without that chip on my shoulder. Some might say it is because I emigrated to Canada in the early 1990s, and I might have to agree to some extent. Back home in the United Kingdom, I ALWAYS felt second-class, all throughout my academic years and the short period I spent there after graduating... I still do, whenever I go back to visit my family. I am British. I was born and bred in Tipton, yet some of MY people didn't accept me, rather I was a foreigner in my own home. My personal journey in the backdrop of Canada has allowed me to erase some of the negativity from the frontal cortex of my brain, and moving it to a sub-folder called the *trash bin!*

The Three Houses

Randomness:

THE FULL HUMAN POTENTIAL...BREAK ON THROUGH.

The analogy of a seedling and its growth can be reflected in the development of an individual. Not the physical from birth to adulthood, but rather the inner growth of oneself.

The seedling is planted with the potential of providing valuable resources when harvested, be that vegetables and fruits or possibly a perennial plant like an Oak tree, for its wood. For the embryonic plant to continue its growth, specific nutrients and essentials from its ecosystem (water, oxygen, and the right temperature) are a necessity for it to break through the soil and to fulfil its full potential.

Similarly, as we mature as individuals, our growth should occur internally in our conscious state of mind. Like the seed, have we managed to break through the dark, damp environment within? Are we pushing to grow beyond the perceived mental and physical barriers?

Let's not forget, not all seeds manage to break through the soil, to escape the cold, damp, dark environment. Similarly, not all of us are able to escape the dark negative environment within our minds.

Illustration 11: The Full Human Potential...Break on Through
by Kulbir Colin Singh Dhillon

So, what does it take for a seed or a human to break on through? I have personally equated it to applying 15% more effort into anything you do...just 15%. Focus on the task or situation at hand and increase your output by 15%. To make that change in your current situation requires a level of focus and dedication; silencing the negative voices within, and not settling for the status quo.

We should all want to mature into that oak tree, to provide multiple purposes for our lives. I have managed to write this book because of my 'additional 15%' theory and breaking through my soil barrier. Trust me, if I can do it, so can you...!

"Break on Through" - (The Doors, 1967)

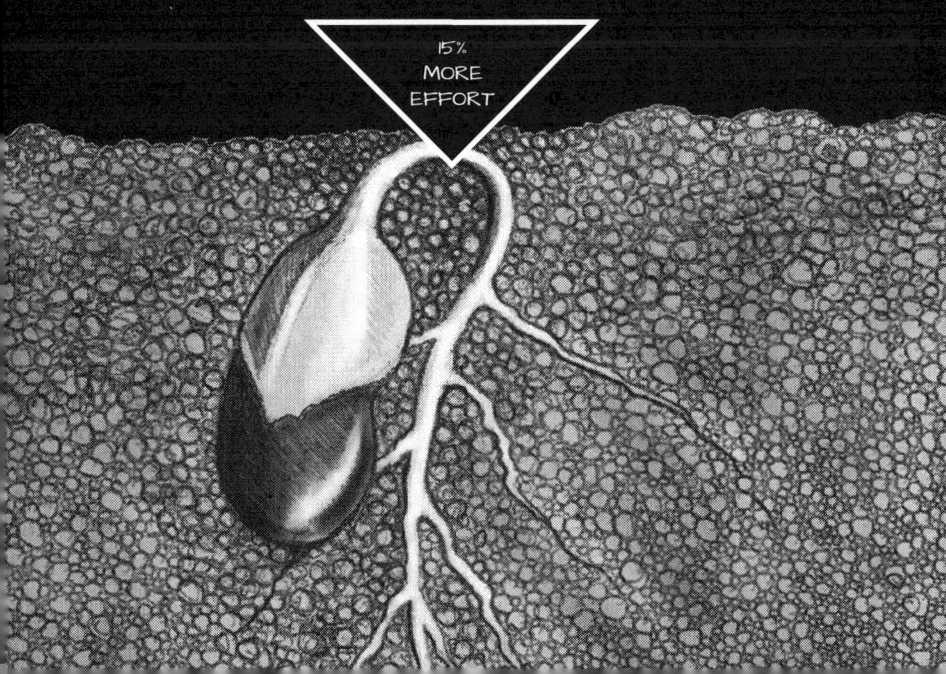

CHAPTER 6

The Brit-Bhangra Generation

As I was growing up, I realized that the integral connection to our rich and colourful *Punjabi* heritage was the culture that shaped our parents. They had brought the key elements along with them when they migrated to the West in the 50s, 60s, and 70s, and in turn, it became part of who we are. *Punjabi* music was a homing beacon for me and my generation.

The Indian community in Britain had settled in three core areas. To the South, Southall was close enough to London, or at least to Heathrow Airport for everyone else to think of it as London. It was the *Punjabi* cultural hub where the *Sikh* community thrived. England has always been historically ruled from the South, and the migrant communities followed this rule instinctively. To the North, the community had settled in less dense pockets in places like Sheffield, Bradford, Manchester, and Liverpool, all the way up to Newcastle. Finally, my family settled in the West

Midlands, an area in the western-central part of England made up of Birmingham, Wolverhampton, Coventry, Dudley, Solihull, Walsall, West Bromwich, and Tipton, to name but a few. My family attended a *Gurdwara* in Coventry. The Aunties and Uncles (culturally we call older ladies, aunties and older men, uncles as a sign of respect) and cousins that made up our extended family also worshipped in the same *Gurdwara*. The rest of the congregation (*Sangat*) of the *Gurdwara* was compiled of people from not just Coventry but Wolverhampton, Southall, Leeds along with other towns and cities in the Midlands.

In the mid/late 1980s, there were at least twenty-two boys at our *Gurdwara*. We were between 15-19 years of age and old enough to shoulder some of the responsibility involved in serving in a *Gurdwara*. We offered free kitchen (*Langar*) on Sundays, serving food up and down the aisles where the congregation was seated. We were young and strong and also took on the heavy-lifting duties of any construction or gardening that was required, and some of us would also rotate with the continuous reading of the *Sikh* prayer called *Japji Sahib* in scheduled two-hour sessions (24/7, Friday-to-Sunday).

We were all adolescents navigating the maze of puberty being bombed by hormonal changes. We did our service in a *Gurdwara* that was fully steeped in our *Sikh* heritage. Our weekends were wrapped up in tradition and duty and stood in sharp contrast to our daily lives which were full-on "British". The contrast was something that most of our parents could never fully comprehend. For them, we simply had to behave and be the next generation of good *Sikh* children. Tradition demanded it of us! Some of us might have challenged the norms occasionally, where we were classified as 'bad boys' and treated as such. Our parents' generation was far from being flawless themselves, yet they expected superhuman perfection from us. We were charged with bringing their dreams and wishes to fruition. Childhood was tough, to say the least. These astronomical expectations added a lot of pressure on all of us. No adult wisely ever suggested that maybe the two cultures colliding together were creating a difficult set of circumstances for the youth, without the added pressure to be model 'Clark Kent' sons and daughters.

When we were not doing selfless service (*Seva*) within the *Gurdwara*, we would find ourselves getting together in one of our parents' cars or later in the cars of some individuals as they became old enough to drive. This environment became our safe haven. We could sit together in the parking lot, talk, laugh, and be ourselves, which included using foul language that was a part of our everyday colourful culture! We could listen to music that was a fusion between Eastern and Western musical traditions called, *Bhangra*, and turn it up to drown out the ribald talking of warm-blooded hormonally charged boys.

As mentioned earlier, in the racially charged atmosphere of the 1970s and 80s, gangs of skinheads were engaging in random and acts of violence on all immigrants. As *Sikhs*, we had always defended others in the name of justice. We did it when we fought

Mughal oppression and turned *Punjab* into the richest Kingdom of its kind in the world, both economically and culturally. We did it when *Sikhs* enlisted in astonishing numbers to fight valiantly in the Great Wars of the World (in the last two world wars, 83,005 turban-wearing *Sikh* soldiers were killed and 109,045 were wounded). We were the descendants of warriors and those racist gangs of hooligans were not about to intimidate us…well not all the time! *Sikhs* began to form gangs of their own. They mobilized and gave themselves names like The *Tutti-Nangs*, The *Gyanis*, and The Holy Smokes. The local vigilantes patrolled the streets and defended the community against the marauding gangs of thugs. Their presence allowed the daily fear of violence to abate and gave rise to a renewed sense of pride in ourselves and our history. Systemic racism continues to be a black mark on Britain even today. In 2020, it seems like not much has truly changed.

Our land of the five rivers, *Punjab*, was a prosperous and fertile basin that fed the nation (even though it was partly because of Monsanto and their fertilizers and pesticides, but that's another story for another day). Our people are as colourful as our history, proud and independent. Our music permeates through our beings. The *Sikh* faith was founded in the 15th Century in Northern India. We have eleven Teachers (*Gurus*) that assisted with the promotion of a monism faith and philosophy. The *Sikh* scriptures are a collection of poems. The first *Guru*, *Guru Nanak Dev Ji*, and his childhood friend, *Mardana*, who carried the five-stringed *rebeck* (*rabab*) as *Guru Ji* sang the couplets of poetry that were his original message of Oneness. Wherever our community has travelled to build a home, our music travelled with us and has rooted us in our culture, no matter how far from *Punjab* we may find ourselves. It may have taken different forms such as singing hymns, praying, meditating to music, or simply enjoying folk, country, and popular music, nonetheless, it is an integral part of our being.

Thanks to *Punjabi* music, also known as *Bhangra*, we shook ourselves free of the pain and hatred thrown at us as we sang and danced. The power of music and singing uplifts the soul and frees the sorrowful mind and body. Our brothers and sisters in slavery used singing and music to strengthen their spirit and resolve.

In 1967, *Dalbir Singh Khanpur* sang a song when he and his brothers founded the group *Bhujangy* in Birmingham. They were the first *Punjabi Bhangra* band to come out of the Midlands and their success lit the way for all those who would follow. What set them apart from anything recorded before was the inclusion of western instruments in playing the pure *Punjabi* lyrical songs. They celebrated the fusion of East and West that had us all in a state of disarray. Music became a bridge between generations and we found something that we could share with our parents to reassure them, even while we were dancing our way out of their comfort zones. *Bhangra* bands like *Alaap* and *Heera* began to climb up the '*desi*' charts (in the 1980s *bhangra* artists were selling over 30,000 cassettes a week, but no artists reached the

top 40 United Kingdom charts, despite outselling popular British bands!) *Malkit Singh*, The *Sahotas, Premi, Apna Sangeet, Shakti*, and *DCS* these bands, were not only being noticed in England, but *Punjabi's* outside of the United Kingdom - Canada, America, and Australia began to purchase their music too.
We were young, inspired, and in the thick of it. Even in our sleepy little *Gurdwara* parking lot. One of us would load the cassette deck with the latest *Bhangra* hit, giving the rest of us the chance to listen to the complete album to see how we liked it. We gave ourselves a name, and the cars we sat in became our mobile offices for organizing the activities of "The Firm". The founder of the group organized a concert, a so-called "Day-Timer" gig, which was a huge success, leading to a series of other live events, and "The Firm" found itself as a bonafide launchpad for upcoming *bhangra* pop stars.

We started with posters to advertise the shows, and because I was the upcoming designer, it fell upon me to sketch out the design of the flyers and posters. The artwork was sketched onto a plain or lined piece of paper using a blue ballpoint pen, and then it would be taken to the printers, where it would be recreated and printed off on bright neon-coloured paper. We built up a network of Asian shopkeepers in key cities who would be willing to keep a stack of the tickets behind their counters. We also rounded up security and volunteers for the actual events.

None of us were over 18. None of us drank alcohol, yet most of our events were held in night clubs and bars. A typical night would have three bands performing with the crowd saving their most exuberant energy for the biggest, most popular band who played at the end. The audience consisted of mostly young men ranging from late teens to late twenties. As time went on, more and more young women began appearing at the shows, but they were always outnumbered by the blokes (4:1). No matter the gender, most of the youths there were without the knowledge or permission of their parents.

The drinking, smoking, and flirting that happened in the clubs was a clear admission of parental failure, as far as the elders were concerned. The revelry and licentiousness were at odds with the religious and cultural grounding that our parents were trying to instill in us.

My parents definitely fit in that category. But mind-bogglingly enough, they never even brought up the fact that they knew of my involvement. They also did not start off as enthusiastic about the music as we were. They were worried that we would be steered into a life of vice and sin. In some cases, they were right. But we were not about to share that information with them.

As time passed and most of us went off to University, in 1990, the organization continued to grow. I became the Asian Society President within my first year at Sheffield Hallam University. This always felt strange, because I grew up with pretty much White folk. I did not choose my friends based on the colour of their skin or their ethnic-religious affiliation. Instead, I have always chosen my friends based on my feelings and emotions. If we clicked...then we were mates. That simple! My only Asian connections had occurred during weekends at the *Gurdwara* or family gatherings.

The President position allowed me to make contacts with other universities and to be able to arrange coaches full of students from all over the UK, to attend our shows.

In the 1990s, we held events at the top night clubs in London, Birmingham, Bradford, Leicester, and Wolverhampton. It allowed us to build relationships and get to know the artists. The *Sahota's* were one particular band that I personally connected with. They were also Black Country lads. Their style of *Bhangra* was a fusion with reggae and synthesized pop. In the summer of 1991, I worked as a double-glazing window salesman, going door-to-door to make sales. Let me tell you, it was not an easy job, but two things made it bearable; one was Matthew's home-made egg salad sandwiches that are made using his secret ingredients (I'm pretty sure it was ground black pepper, but all in all, they were really tasty) and the other was working along with *Kash Sahota*, the drummer from the *Sahota's*.

Being successful promoters also put us in jeopardy when our success drew the kind of attention we really did not want. Our promoting days came crashing down after death threats and being jacked, soured the taste of success!

Our last concert in the town of Wolverhampton was at the new night club called Foxes. We had been using the same security firm to keep order at all our shows for many years. They were really friendly with the founder of The Firm. going to his house for social visits between shows. On the day of any given show, it was a part of my responsibility to collect the money. I emptied the cash registers and I also collected from the organizers of all the coaches. The money would be kept on me for the entire evening. I never feared being attacked or held up. I carried myself with an air of confidence and a look that simply said, "You do not want to f@#k with me!"

On this particular day in 1992, two of our senior security members came rushing out of the club with The Firm's founder. They ran past the reception area where I was, and they hurriedly asked me to come along with them. At this point, I had no clue about what was going on and so, I went along. We made for the car, one of the security guys jumped behind the wheel and I sat in the front passenger seat. My colleague and the other security guy sat in the back. Even before sitting in the car, I knew something was terribly wrong. The atmosphere was thick and adverse and the body language from the security guards was hostile. I knew that my colleague and I needed to show a united front in this situation. As soon as the car was started, accusations started being hurled. They were clearly fabricated to create a situation. What was actually going down was a "tax". The two goons were attempting extortion. The one in the back asked for the money collected that night.

My colleague replied, "I don't have any."
At that point, the bouncer leaned over and tapped my breast pocket.

"Here it is."

All the while the car was moving. We were being driven to a very shady part of town to further the intimidation. The voices in the car began to get even louder. They menacingly told us how they were disappointed in us and how now we were going to pay the price. I will be quite honest; I was a wee bit nervous. I knew they wanted the cash, but I did not know what they would do with us after getting it. I had my wits about me and knew that we had the edge in speed, and I used that certainty to calm myself down.

The security goons were over six feet tall. One was over 300lbs and the other around 220lbs. They eventually realized that we were going to be muscled into giving up the cash. We never wanted to make trouble, especially from two characters like them. I handed over all the cash, and the death threats stopped. We ended up being dropped off at the side of the road about four miles away from the nightclub.

Maybe "The Firm" had reached its peak as an organization that was beginning to get more popularity without a formalized organizational structure! We started something as amateurs, passionate about creating something new and exciting while remaining at the heart of this movement. Although we enjoyed what we did, the attack at Foxes was a turning point. This was a hobby for most of us, not a long-term career option. So, it was time to move on.

From 1988 to 1992, The Firm served its purpose. It was responsible for some of the most successful, well-organized *Bhangra* shows in Britain. We were consistently hosting the top British *Bhangra* bands of the two decades. These shows played an essential part in the growth of the British *Bhangra* scene. What seemed to be simply a great way of making money paved the way for British *Bhangra* to become an international phenomenon. In reflection, I see that our efforts, entrepreneurship, drive, and our wanting to be a part of the British *Bhangra* music scene made a substantive difference in how *Punjabi* music was perceived by the mainstream, not only in the United Kingdom but also in North America and yes, even in India. We played our part in bringing the heartbeat of *Punjab* back to where it belonged, and we had put an anglicized piece of ourselves in it.

The Brit-*Bhangra* movement not only paved the path to connect us to a part of our rich heritage, but it also gave some of our parents a sense of comfort in knowing that we were not completely lost to the "Mainstream British" pop culture. The party scene may not have been the path they wanted us to follow, but it was a step towards safeguarding our heritage.

Randomness:

INFLUENTIAL MUSICAL ARTISTS.

The universal language is how it has been described, and to be honest, it can only be interpreted that way. Music penetrates all borders, crosses cultural boundaries, and does not require a translator. You certainly will know if you like what you hear or not. The sounds and their vibrations given off by the instruments, resonate through us and can connect us with that energy source which is the REAL U.

Whether you are listening to an instrumental melody performed by an orchestra in one of the finest auditoriums, or simply watching a YouTube channel with a young musician doing an 'acoustic cover' version of their favourite artist's latest offering; if you let it, the sounds will take you to a good place, letting your mind wander and sometimes...lift you up to higher realms.

My list of musical artists come together from different nations and genres. The resounding similarity that most of my artists have in common is their lyrics. It is what I call 'meaningful' lyrics; a subject matter that is being sung tends to be for the betterment of all those that listen. Just as Paul McCartney once said about the Beatles, I paraphrase, "We sing about love". Both love and spirituality will get you on my playlist. On the other hand, when I am working out, there is nothing better than an intense score from a motion picture, or a classic rap ballad filled with profanity of the highest order ...universal languages.

Michael Jackson – *Shakti* – *Nusrat Fateh Ali Khan* – The Beatles – *Bhai Harjinder Singh, Sri Nagar Wale* - Mumford and Sons - Elvis Presley – Tracy Chapman - Led Zeppelin - The Doors - Lionel Richie - The Safri Boyz - *Malkit Singh* – Run DMC - Cliff Richard – Bob Dylan - George Harrison – Hans Zimmer - Oasis – Queen – U2 – Alaap - Howard Shore - Bob Marley

A. R. Rahman – *Amrinder Gill* - Dr. Dre – George Michael - *Kanwar Grewal* – N.W.A - Pink Floyd - The Police – Sam Cooke - R.E.M – Elton John - Public Enemy - Simon & Garfunkel - Roy Orbison Neil Young - *Apna Sangeet* - *Heera* - *Achanak* - Shin & DCS – John Lennon - Bee Gees - Depeche Mode – Drake - Grandmaster Flash - INXS - Jay-Z - Linkin Park - Peter Gabriel - Peter Cetera - *Raman Djawadi* - Rhianna - *Sukshinder Shinda* - Simple Minds - *Sonu Nigam* – Tupac

Illustration 12: Tabla by Kulbir Colin Singh Dhillon

THE THREE HOUSES·THE THREE HOUSES·

THE BUILDING YEARS

Map of the Black Country. UK

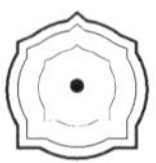

CHAPTER 7
Rivers of Blood

I was born in England but never felt English. However, I do have a Black Country-Brummie accent, but maybe my skin tone and appearance are too ethnic. Maybe I am a second-class Englishman. Maybe this is why I felt the way I did, and I am sure others who are reading this book may have sensed this "less than" feeling being projected by peers, their friend's parents, the average construction workers, employees in shops, and even some of our educators too. Don't forget that I grew up in a post - Peter Griffiths and Enoch Powell Britain, where the 'Rivers of Blood' were already apparently flowing. In 1968, these ludacris politicians dare to sharply criticize the immigration of Commonwealth immigrants, taunting the parents of those children I would befriend, to stand-up and take action before Britain becomes a cesspool and its culture is wiped out. Really? Peter Griffiths, the conservative MP for Smethwick, about 4 miles from Tipton, won a seat with a slogan; "If you want a n***er for a neighbour, vote Labour". He would proudly share with those who asked, how his daughter came up with that vile catchphrase. Remember, in the late 1950s signs outside businesses and residences said, "No Blacks, Irish, and Dogs Allowed". Though the signs were taken down by the 60s, the attitudes firmly stayed up! The news of Peter Griffiths travelled across the globe and the American activist, *Malcolm X arrived in England to show support for the visible minorities. I remember uncle, *Avtar Singh Johal*, a senior member of the then Indian Workers Association, and a family relative, sharing the story with my dad about how they invited Malcolm X to Smethwick. Malcolm's presence brought attention to the segregation in pubs and racism, people of colour had to endure. What about the Roman invasions from AD 50 to AD 400, the Nordic Vikings invasions AD 800 to AD 1066, or the Norman conquest. People of colour and unique ethnic cultures have been a staple ingredient in Britain, specifically England's long history, but maybe their skin tones were lighter and therefore more acceptable. Maybe the ingredients in their cooking didn't give off such a potent smell. Or maybe the visitors from thousands of years ago were also made to feel unwelcomed. Does Brexit confirm my thoughts and feelings? Did British residents vote on leaving the EU or a want for a certain group of NEW immigrants to leave their shores? You know my feelings on this already...

---

*Nine days later, on February 21st, 1965, Malcolm X would be assassinated at the Audubon Ballroom in New York. The world would lose this giant of a man!

Is my outlook a projection tarnished by the dreadful stories of the partition of India, passed down from my parents and grandparents? The stories of *Sikh* struggles began when tens of thousands were massacred because Cyril Radcliffe, the cartographer who had never stepped foot east of Paris, France, however under the guidance of Viceroy Mountbatten, decided to draw lines of blood and segregate a people from their faith's foundation and old capital City of *Lahore*. Did these historical events that my parents shared cloud my personal outlook when I was faced with a racial or prejudiced situation growing up... maybe? Or did they put them into context!

Primary school was, in most part, a healthy experience; high school had the potential to traumatize me, especially for the first two years. My friends couldn't comprehend some of my experiences. I was never expecting them to since the vast majority were predominately White Anglo Saxon Protestants (WASP). Some of you will think that I should have befriended some of my own community - safety in numbers and all of that, but I'm not wired that way. You are a friend of mine because of what we have in common, our likes and dislikes, the jokes we laugh at, the way you see others, treat others. Colour, race, and faith have always been irrelevant.

High school had its challenges. Emotionally, I only had my brother to share some of the horrors I went through. I could only imagine they were a scratch on the surface of what he, the first and only turban-wearing individual in 1981 would have gone through. Did I sometimes, as a child, wish I was born white? The answer is yes. Did I sometimes, as a child, wish I didn't have to carry this burden of faith that was so physically different from the Judaeo-Christian beliefs that others practiced? Yes. Did I feel that maybe I was being punished for past-life impurities? Yes. Should a child have to think and feel this way? NO.

Life at University began with a trip to Canada the summer before school started. It was a summer with my maternal uncle, my *Mama Ji* (late *Tara Singh Randhawa*), and his family. Those four weeks in the Toronto area changed my life. I felt like I belonged here – it felt like home. I also travelled the east coast of the United States on a Greyhound coach with my final destination being Florida. The United States portion of the journey confirmed that Canada was going to be my future home. It has the new world feeling, big city trimmings like the United States, but it felt like home…the air tasted familiar, the pace of life seemed similar. Why? Because for those four weeks of being a tourist, a visitor, and some days no different than local Canadians, not for once did I feel…*second class. No one called me a *Paki*, nobody looked at me, my turban and made a racial remark, either to my face or under their breath. I remember going to a large shopping mall to look for it, to identify someone within the mall looking at me through racially tinted glasses. It didn't happen. Let me put this into context. Trust me, I'm not exaggerating when I say this, I hadn't travelled anywhere within the United Kingdom and not faced some level of racism… nowhere. Sad, I know!

At university, my colleagues and fellow students in Industrial Design were predominately white. Still, those that I lived with, ate with, and laughed with were Muslim, *Sikh*, *Hindu*, not forgetting my closest friend, Dave 'Scouser' Colligan. We used to call our group the UN. These friendships and relationships were more profound and more substantial than possibly any other that I had experienced before. When one lives with other people, shares the challenges of student life, including financial, social, and emotional struggles, oftentimes very little is hidden. Once university was over, I worked a summer job to earn some money to help me begin my new life in Canada, and then I was off… did I look back? Yes, I did several times. But why wouldn't I? My family were all back home in Blighty.

Life in Canada began in the fall of 1993. I arrived on the day the Blue Jays were going to celebrate their second world series with a parade in downtown Toronto. I had already facsimiled my resume and a two-page portfolio overview to a number of design consultancies in the Toronto area. I came to make Canada my home - from Tipton to Toronto.

---

*I understand entirely how Sikhs and other minorities have felt second-class in Canada's recent history. In 1914, a ship called the Komagata Maru carrying 376 passengers (the vast majority Sikhs) was not allowed to dock in Vancouver, British Columbia, Canada due to the racist Canadian Continuous Journey Act. How Canadian law racially discriminated against the Indigenous people of Canada, and some will argue that it continues to do so today. Like other nations, Canada has a lot of work to do around race relations but let me be frank...we are a beacon of hope for the world to glance at and admire.

THE THREE HOUSES·THE THREE HOUSES·

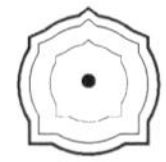

CHAPTER 8

Love Marriage Arranged

The essence of love and the cosmic energy we call God are in fact the same. It can be described as formless, timeless, and unconditional. Faiths believe in a higher power that cultivates a mutual relationship between you and your deity, are all based upon love. Now, take that love and apply it to a physical person. It can be an individual that is of this earth and present with you, someone like yourself. Put that love into a relationship you build and develop and the results can be spiritually uplifting. The unconditional love that recognizes no time barriers and takes form in the partner you have for your life's journey. My love's name is *Satinderjit Kaur Dhillon.* I call her Cindy. Let me share with you our "*Bollywood*" love story.

Have you ever watched an Indian *Bollywood* movie? Until recently, the vast majority of the movies had to include the following content; a tragic love story, a villain, a romantic scene normally staged on a mountain top, with the hero wearing a shady sweater and the heroine prancing around in a *sari*, and lots of excessive fight scenes with exaggerated sound effects.

The love stories depicted in the films challenged the cultural norms of the Indian subcontinent. Marriages were arranged and you could be disowned for choosing your life partner. Arranged marriages for the most part were the bringing together of not just two individuals but more so, two families. As the old African saying goes, "It takes a village to raise a child", it takes possibly two villages to arrange a marriage. If you were lucky, you would be able to meet your future partner once, just for a short conversation, before you had to make the commitment. The response that the family elders were looking for was a 'yes'. Why? Because the middleman had done the leg work in determining whether or not the two families were a match, the two individuals were typically secondary to that equation!

In 1992, my parents started telling me to be prepared for marriage the following year. My brother was married at twenty-one and I was expected to have an arranged marriage soon after I graduated from University. The thought of spending the rest of my life with someone I did not know was scary, but then you only had to look around you. My brother, cousins, and close family all had arranged marriages and they all seemed to be happy and content. Truth be told, one of the reasons for fleeing the UK at the time was to avoid marriage. However, when I arrived in Canada I ran right into Cindy. We did not find ourselves on a mountain top wearing some questionable, inappropriate non-mountain climbing gear, but we did have the first love marriage in our families' history!

I am not sure if I truly understand or believe in the premise of destiny. Do I believe that our every thought and move is already planned? Are we simply chugging along on spiritual rail tracks that have been laid down by our maker? Surely, we are more than mere rail carriages packed full of pre-programmed traits. One thing that I do believe to be true is that our thoughts, when truly felt, become the energy that can transcend geographical boundaries and cross oceans and seas to manifest themselves.

As mentioned in the previous chapter, I first visited Canada in the summer of 1990. At the time, I was nineteen years old. Before heading back home to England from that brief visit, I promised myself and my Maternal Uncle that after finishing university, I would move to Canada permanently. I eventually did this, but circumstances changed the potential outcome and manner in which I arrived. In 1992, My *Mama Ji* was diagnosed with cancer and was told he had less than 12 months to live. On the 23rd of October 1993, I arrived in Canada to keep my promise and to spend time with him before that opportunity was taken away from me.

During the three years, preceding my arrival in Canada, I had exchanged several letters, by mail, with my cousin, *Hardeep*. We talked about many things in our correspondence. This was before email became a means of digital communication or even before the internet was widely available. Our topics of intercontinental conversation would include girls. I was in my early 20s and he was younger than me and eloquent in writing his romantic wishes. He told me about a girl he knew would be a perfect match for me. "I'll introduce you to her when you come back to Canada for good", he said.

I was a *Sardar*; A turban-wearing *Sikh* boy with unshorn hair. I did not think of myself as attractive to the opposite sex. I know this because I rarely had girls express even the remotest interest in me. I did not drink or smoke. For most of my life, I was a vegetarian. Truth is, I was pretty boring. Girls found me to be two-dimensional in comparison to the bad boys that they liked. I also did not have a great deal of self-confidence when it came to girls. That was probably knocked out of me by Skinheads or the fact that I was brought up to treat all girls like sisters (it's a cultural thing). Remember, I grew up in a time where you could leave the house feeling pretty good about yourself, and out of the blue, "*Paki*" would be hurled at you, just to remind you of your precarious standing in British society. That word would send you right back into the hole that they assumed you had crawled out of. It worked miracles for taking the wind out of your sails. It left you feeling flat and adrift and in no position to charm a bloody seagull, let alone a girl. Plus, I had high standards. I was not about to settle for any girl. I was looking for someone that was physically beautiful, strong, and intelligent!

There is something about travelling that allows you a level of freedom, which you may not feel at home, and the sense of adventure that comes with it. I enjoyed everything about Canada. The people, the layout of the major cities, and the fact that the place looked so clean and well planned it made me love the country even more. It was December 1993 and my cousin, *Hardeep*, and I were at Shopper's World, a mall in the suburb of the City of Brampton, Ontario. We strolled past an electronic store when Hardeep stopped me in my tracks.

"Wait. Wait! That's her!" he said with one hand on my chest stopping me from moving forward. His body stretched out, looking around the corner and into the store.

"Who?" I asked.

"You remember that girl that I told you about in the letters: The one that went to my school. The one whose younger sister is in my grade!! That's HER!!"

I moved forward and peered past him to see if I could make out which girl he was talking about. But there were a lot of people in the store.

"Which one?", I asked.

He pointed out the one with the long brown silky hair and the brown jacket. I stepped back. She was beautiful; absolutely stunning. I leaned against the wall while *Hardeep* went into the store to speak to her. There was no way that I was going to follow him in, but part of me wanted to stop him before he even reached her. The thought of being rejected and humiliated, not only back home but now also on another continent, was not sitting well. My stomach began to turn. Should I go after him, to stop him? Instead, I concentrated on steadying my breathing and waited for Hardeep to re-emerge. He did and brought the attractive girl with him.

Our Introduction

"Cindy, meet your future husband, Colin. Colin, meet your future wife, Cindy", said *Hardeep*. Those lines were the ice breaker introduction.

She smiled and reached out her hand. She did not appear to be phased by Hardeep's proclamation in the least; rather she laughed at the sum of his introduction. However, we shook hands. Now history had put me at this juncture several times. No, not being introduced to my future wife, but meeting a girl that I might have thought to be attractive. The next step from what seemed to be a pleasant first meeting was…nothing. No reaction that I could gauge to tell that I had even a remote chance to continue to the flirting phase. If she showed any reaction at all, it was normally what I called the "Brother" look which kids today call the 'Friend Zone'. Boy, oh boy, did I ever own that zone! But Cindy's reaction, her smile, her body language, and now that I think of it, her aura/energy level, was welcoming. I smiled back, looking at her, then down towards my feet and a slight glance at her again.

We made some pleasantries and then left. *Hardeep* skipped in front of me and asked what I thought of the meeting. I told him she was far more beautiful in person than his descriptions had led me to visualize. He assured me that she liked me too. I might have said that I agreed but internally, I doubted it very much. There were very few turban-wearing *Sikh* boys in the 80s and 90s. Our generation was trying to 'fit into' western culture by sacrificing some of the outer features of our faith. Wearing a turban was not seen as 'cool', rather it stereotyped you as being backward…old-fashioned, and religious.

Punjabi Sikh girls preferred a clean-shaven *Sikh* over a turban-wearing *Sikh*. The clash between religious and cultural practices are quite glaring. As a practicing *Sikh*, one would refrain from intoxicants and any product that could be labelled addictive or a drug. Culturally though, *Punjabis* are known to drink like fish!

Though the vast majority of male *Sikhs* used to adorn a turban when they left India in the 1900s and began to settle in new continents, but some *Sikhs* decided to assimilate and cut their hair, as mentioned in an earlier chapter. My family had been practicing *Sikhs* since the mid-1970s. My father, brother, and I wore turbans and had unshorn hair.

I left Britain to live in Canada permanently, this was going to be my new home. I sent out copies of my resume and facsimile versions of my best portfolio pieces to several design consultancies in the Toronto area. I spoke to them on the phone before being offered an interview. To be honest, a few of them said they were interested in what they saw. My history made me sensitive to different attitudes, regarding the way I looked. Due to my appearance, I was treated differently, even here in Canada. I would appear for my interview and suddenly, the atmosphere would change. I do not know if it was subtle racism, or my sixth sense kicking in from my past experiences!

Interview after interview, I was being told, "Thank you. We will let you know". The reception at the interviews was always cold. As soon as they would open the door and see me, a turban-wearing *Sikh*, right then I could sense from their body language and response, that I might as well turn around and go back home, but I wanted to stay in Canada. I wanted Toronto to be my new home. My *Mama Ji* and I discussed options; and considering the design profession, specifically, the small design consultancies were being run by groups of white Canadians, who might see me as a social threat to daily-life and social norms in their small companies, I decided that I had to make a choice. Either cut my hair and stop wearing my turban or change my career path to something more general, where I would blend in. Having been a target of racism and bullying my entire life, I just wanted to begin a new life. I was exhausted with always having to fight a battle with both myself and what felt like the rest of the world.

Yes, I was not being targeted by blunt racial comments, or being physically assaulted by racist thugs, which certainly made Canada more attractive, but the subtle non-acceptance of my physical appearance was still prevalent - I felt it.

Now wanting to cut my hair and doing it were polar opposites. First, I needed to ask the permission of my parents. Yes, I was in my early twenties but see, culturally, we have that respectful relationship with our parents where their opinion matters. How was I going to pluck up the courage to have that conversation with my Dad? The thought of cutting my hair did make me sick to my stomach. The history of my people was littered with atrocities and massacres. Values were once put on the head of a *Sikh*, and why? Because we had always stood up to the face of tyranny and oppression. We have given our lives for the freedom of religion and speech, and that included everyone's religion, not just ours!

I couldn't muster up the courage needed to talk directly to my Dad. Rather, I asked my *Mama Ji* to do this for me. Surprisingly, I was given the go-ahead. Though I was about to change my appearance, I had promised myself and my parents that the change was a temporary one so that I could do something different. Once I was settled, I would keep my hair again and place that crown we call a turban, back onto my head.

I met Cindy as a turban-wearing *Sikh* and that was extremely important to me. I was glad she liked that I looked like a textbook *Sikh*. The following day, after meeting Cindy, I cut my hair and trimmed down my beard. *Hardeep* was running an errand that stormy winter afternoon at the local shopping plaza when he bumped into Cindy and her sister. He told Cindy that I was about to cut my hair while getting a ride back home. I came out of the house to meet them and I knew then that whatever was developing between Cindy and me was already very different from anything I had ever experienced before.

Within days, Cindy and I met again, and we began to chat over the telephone. We would talk for several hours a day. I shared all my feelings and poured out the essence of who I was to her. She listened; she's an excellent listener! I had found my life partner, my other half. I know it sounds very cliché but how else do I describe it? I knew that she was the ONE. She was everything that I had ever wanted in a partner. She was stunningly beautiful, and she carried herself confidently. Her voice was soothing and comforting, it felt right! The more we engaged with one another, the more I began to realize why I was the *iron filings* being attracted to this electromagnetic being. Her beauty came from within, it radiated outwardly and her aura was strikingly luminescent.

The new year arrived, it was 1994, and within weeks of meeting each other, both Cindy and I knew that this was it. But this was 1994, not 2020, at a time when marriages were arranged for us, not by us. Love marriages were rare and not well-received in the *Punjabi-Sikh* community. I had gone against my faith and cut my hair. I had gone against my culture and found my soul mate and had yet to tell my parents. I did not have the courage to break this news to them, and once again *Mama Ji* did this for me. I was shocked when the response came back in a letter written by my brother on behalf of my parents. They said that if we, Cindy and I were happy and understood it was a life-long commitment, then we had their blessings. I was speechless! I absolutely did not expect that kind of response. I kept waiting for a second letter that would be the one to express their true dismay, but it never arrived.

The next stage was to announce our relationship to Cindy's parents. She was the oldest of three and as such, she bore the extra burden of always having to do the right thing, to set a good example for her younger siblings. The conversation took place between Cindy and her mother on the stairs leading down to the basement. Unbeknownst to them both, Cindy's Dad was sitting upstairs in the family room which was right at the top of those stairs. Their voices were loud enough where he overheard pretty much the entire conversation. Cindy's parents were not as accepting of the situation, and they asked that she refrain from making the mistake of seeing me again. When my *Mami Ji* (Maternal uncle's wife) called Cindy's house to talk about the next steps leading up to our betrothal, Cindy's Mom declined and told her not to ring back.

Our dire situation was calling out for the infamous "Middleman", the matchmaker in order to assure that the conditions of the protocol were met in full. We began the search for a *Bachola*!

Socially, in India, all or most marriages have a *Bachola* involved. He or she brings the two families together by providing a kind of neutral zone. The *Bachola* has to be someone known and trusted by both families. The two families used to stay apart through the whole process of wedding preparations, up to the wedding day itself. All communication is done strictly through the Bachola. As a result of this important role the *Bachola* plays in communicating details of some very delicate negotiations, it is imperative that both families are able to trust this person. Fortunately for Cindy and me, we both came from the same geographical area back in the *Punjab*, India. Our ancestral villages were less than 5 km away from each other. Finding a link that knew both of our families would not be impossible, even in the Canadian suburb of Brampton. My *Mama Ji* knew of such a family, at which point, *Mama Ji* and *Mami Ji* approached them and asked to formally represent us as the *Bachola*, and reach out to Cindy's family. An agreement that a potential match could be possible was negotiated with the middleman. He contacted Cindy's parents, who then consented to take the next step in this intricate process. You see, when a known individual makes a request, such as this, the situation changes, it becomes a matter of respect and honour. Cindy's parents agreed to meet me in person. A meeting was arranged to introduce her family to mine in a neutral location ...you guessed right, the bachola's house. I arrived with my Mami Ji, Cindy's side of the family included her grandparents and her parents. The meeting went well. They liked what they heard and saw... the ball was rolling.

One Sunday morning, I was sitting in Mama Ji's room reading a magazine, while he rested in bed, suddenly, he called me over. As I came across to the left-hand side of his bed and kneeled to ask what he would like, he asked to see a picture of Cindy. He wanted to see a photograph of the girl that his nephew had become smitten by. I went down to the basement and came back with a picture. I sat on the edge of his bed and I remember the blinds in his room partially closed but were turned upwards so that shafts of light pushed their way into the room, providing rays of light that were soft and warm. When I reached over and showed him the picture, he called me close to him and gently said,

"Call your *Mami Ji*".

I got up and went downstairs to call her. When she came into the bedroom, he showed her the picture of Cindy and said,

"The girl from the pharmacy..."
Mami Ji looked at the picture, then said, "Oh, is this her?"

Mama Ji nodded.

Cindy used to work part-time at a local pharmacy. *Mama Ji* was a frequent customer at the pharmacy, collecting medication and being served by her, and he had said on several occasions, "That girl in the pharmacy would be a good match for *Kulbir*". He knew that she was the one for me even before I had met her. I shared this story with my Mum and that cemented any doubts or concerns she may have had. If her brother said that this was a good thing, then his word was all the assurance she needed to give her blessings.

The date was set, April 30th, 1994, marriage plans were rushed because we wanted to have my *Mama Ji* present for the ceremony, but we lost him on the 5th of April, just a few weeks before our wedding date. He was truly a special soul, a beautiful person, and someone I still miss to this day. He gave me the warmth and comfort of my parents, the trust of a friend, and the knowledge of a teacher. I feel extremely blessed and fortunate to have spent time with him.

What unfolded was overwhelming. I was about to get married. It was a love marriage. I was the first of my clan to do such a thing, and I am pretty sure all my aunties and uncles were over the moon, because it now opened the doors for their children. The fact that my parents had been so accepting is something I never really understood up to this day. I totally expected a different reaction to both, me cutting my hair and the love marriage, I guess they had accepted that I was no longer a boy, but a young man who had jumped continents, and that I too had to make my own decisions in the same ways that they had to when they moved from their homeland, *Punjab*, India to the UK.

In April 2019, Cindy and I celebrated our 25th wedding anniversary. We have two beautiful children, both arrived as 8lbs, 2oz, and 22.5 inch parcels of love and potential, 5 years apart. My son was born in 2000. He was the first man-child in the extended *Dhillon* family, after nearly two decades. This was culturally a joyous occasion for both my family and the extended family.

My daughter was born in 2005, she proudly carries the DNA of the *Dhillon* females. They complete my family. The idiosyncrasies and personality types that help to forge the energy of one's home are radiated through each member's personality. I am a disciplinarian. Cindy is too, but she is also our mother goose; loving, and caring. My son, *Pavitar*, is calm and content, whereas my daughter, *Veerah* is intense and strong-willed: but both are being taught to be good citizens of planet earth, above all.

The four of us have been on many of life's expeditions together and travelled to many exotic places all over the world. Each vacation, each spiritual retreat is a virtual education. We try and soak up the cultural learning of every country we visit. Cindy and I have lived in a basement apartment and we have also owned a ten-acre farm. The journey of life has been filled with ups and downs, but let me tell you about my co-pilot, Cindy.

I am fortunate to have my life partner who has known herself to the very depth of her core. You cannot underestimate the true value of knowing yourself. One of the challenges with "internal investigation" is that, as a society, we do not do enough of it, nor do we place enough value on this practice. How can you truly know another if you do not know yourself? You may not think that it is necessary to really know who you are, but how can you forge relationships without knowing this? Relationships are based on commonalities and grass-root connections between two people, but are these connections aligned, or do you just think they are? Cindy is one of those individuals that know their true self. It is what allows her to radiate and literally light up rooms, homes, and workspaces. Her philosopher stone personality helps to better those around her, IF they choose.

Don't get me wrong, life was not always perfect, life today is not always impeccable! We have our differences. We are both strong personalities, but our common ground is that we are committed to our relationship. We both know that the grass is never greener on the other side, in fact, it is usually a slight shade of yellow.

Our first few years of marriage witnessed many episodes of two individuals trying to lay down his/her conditions; their wants and desires for the other. We were both quite young, which I believed, helped the situation. Our minds and hearts were not hardened by individualism or by societal expectations. Though we would put our foot down and took stands when in a dispute, we both still had the potential to admit when we might have been wrong or did not see the situation from the other's perspective, which in fact might have been the better viewpoint. I came into the marriage with some of the cultural bias, that I was the man and what I said was the law. Whereas Cindy has some strong feminist views of equality, which were fairly new to the *Punjabi* culture. As time progressed, I learned that some of my views were outdated and it shouldn't be that way. What was best for any given situation, in our relationship, was a shared decision-making process, despite whose idea it was, as this thought process always ensured the best outcome. As difficult and painful as that process might have been, I can truly say that we have both kept each other in check, and we still do to this day.

The global journey's that I have been on, have given me many opportunities to see and experience various cultures and people, these experiences have only confirmed one thing for me internally; it simply confirmed that Cindy is a beautiful being. A pure soul that exudes love and calmness. I initially fell for her looks and those exotic-kind eyes. I am blessed daily with her compassion and warmth. She was my self-help guide even before I picked up any one of those self-improvement books. I remember reading Rhonda Byrne's, *The Secret*, and thinking, "This book is about my other half."

The pollination of one's body and mind are critical for a wholesome life and pleasant journey. The act of marriage is a socially accepted ritual that recognizes the union between two individuals, and obligations to any future offspring. The relationship should be built on a solid foundation of love and respect. Could I possibly reach out and suggest that Thomas Jefferson's writings in the American 'Declaration of Independence', could also refer to personal relationships?

> *"We hold these truths to be self-evident: that all men are created equal; that they are endowed by their Creator with certain inalienable rights; that among these are life, liberty, and the pursuit of happiness."*

The pursuit of happiness is an integral part of that journey, and you must hone your craft, not as individual entities, but rather as a team, and I hope that all people might find their yin, to your yang, like a Cindy. I will share a few adjectives and nouns hoping to describe her so that you too can begin to appreciate why I am blessed to be with her;

Affectionate, attentive, attractive, beautiful, beloved, blessed, bright, bubbly, calm, caring, cheerful, courageous, dedicated, devout, disciplined, elegant, emotional, enchanting, fair, feminine, generous, gifted, gorgeous, graceful, grounded, helpful, high-energy, innocent, irreplaceable, kind-hearted, loving, mature, natural, patient, personable, polite, positive, pretty, radiant, ravishing, remarkable, romantic, sacrificing, self-confident, sensitive, sharp, smart, social, special, talkative, thankful, trustworthy, understanding, virtuous, warm-hearted, wise, youthful, achiever, advocate, best friend, caregiver, feminist, fighter, headstrong, hostess, inspirational, intellectual, kind soul, leader, life coach, lioness, mom, natural beauty, optimist, provider, stunner, thinker, wife, and a woman of her word.

If each one of those was a battery-pack or a storage device of electromagnetic energy, you should begin to understand why she is such a special individual in my life. Her bank of positive energy and love is both vast and rechargeable. Do not get me wrong, I have been hearing this for two decades all over the continents. Her magnetism attracts accolades from all types of people, whether they are family, friends, or strangers. Her energy is of the pure kind, it is giving and just. She is respected and admired within her circle of friends (420), and her work colleagues alike. I guess a lot of us are, but her character and integrity are steadfast, she is sincere to honesty and love, in all that she is and does. She does not surround herself with people for the sake of company, rather she is content within her own world and only invites those that will hopefully make it a better place. Her sixth sense; her ability to read people, being able to know and feel who is genuine and who is not, is a wonderful gift.

As individuals, we are both quite different when it comes to personalities. There is a saying "opposites attract". To an extent maybe, but the core philosophy and outlook on life must be the same. If I am punctual, and a stickler for wanting to be on time, then she is infamous for never being on time. Though I am a social bee, I tend to only open up about topics I am passionate about. Cindy, nope! She can adapt herself to all situations and just be herself. We are both disciplinarians, possibly firmer than your average Canadian parents. The difference between us and the previous generation's rules and regulations on discipline is, the loving and natural nurturing inclinations that Cindy is blessed with. I was raised in a house with two strong disciplinarians too, yet someone forgot to read the book on providing some soft, gentle nurturing love (kids should be seen but not heard...). Today, I am possibly lacking in that department, though softening as the years go by, fortunately for me, Cindy is not. She glides between being firm and easy-going, between being direct and casual, with both of our children. This, I feel, provides the home environment with the tangible guidelines that build the foundation of a healthy family.

The Indian/*Punjabi* culture is a collectivistic society promoting the joint family structure, the extended family model. It can provide a nurturing environment for children, and an excellent setting for the love and care of senior family members as well. Our homes were more harmonized than dysfunctional. All family members seemed to be ready to cooperate and collectively resolve any concerning issues, rather than letting them become divisional and bitter. It wasn't until later in life I realized, our homes were based upon a strong matriarchal family model, where the eldest female was the real head of the family. I am pointing this out because the Indian/*Punjabi* society also supports a male chauvinistic culture. The men would be seen as the heads of the family, but in fact, it was typically our grandmothers or mothers that were paramount in the decision-making at home.

Cindy's maternal grandmother, is who we lovingly called, *Bebe*. She was the embodiment of a matriarch; towering stature, firm voice, she always said exactly what she felt - a multi-faceted personality and very loving. When I joined the family, I, along with my parents, instantly fell in love with her. It was no surprise that Cindy was very close to *Bebe*. From a very young age, *Bebe* helped to provide a nurturing environment for Cindy, her family, and the extended family at large. In September 2010, *Bebe* passed away. I have since joked that Cindy has taken up that matriarchal position of her grandmother, even though her mother and her aunties are still alive, and much older. See, Cindy is a driving force, a visionary and someone, much like *Bebe*, who brings the family together. She has a natural capacity to happily adapt to her surroundings and environment. Child-like with the more youthful members, and composed with those that are a bit older than her, she is the energy source within her surroundings. She is not happy to just simply sit back and not be a part of the action. That is not who she is.

This book entails the journey of an individual; a short-list of selected life experiences, hoping to connect with a vast selection of readers, offering you, the reader, an insight into a fellow human being that has ancestry in Northern India. An individual that was born and bred in England, but calls Canada his home. Some will enjoy the funnier and slightly non-politically correct stories; others will bond with the deeper and less foolish aspects of me as an individual. The complete spectrum of events and learning are the foundation of what I called in the preface and the title of this book, *The Three Houses*. All roads must lead to this chapter. Why? Because one must see the transformation and development of oneself, and sometimes this can be experienced through the words of another.

With age, I have matured; through life-experiences, I have ripened; but the photosynthesis of all things positive and wholesomeness have been brought upon by my life partner, Cindy. *The Three Houses* will talk about Contentment, Commitment, and Contribution. They are but a reflection of who I have been drawn to, and whom I have devoted my life to, and I know she feels the same way too.

Life is an independent journey that we all must experience individually, but having a companion to share the journey with, makes the ride that much more exciting, why? Because we are each other's mirror, and a mirror never lies. We work on ourselves by being honest with each other.

Do we agree on all things? Hell no! Has the last twenty-seven years been smooth sailing? No! Do we share the same tastes in food, music, movies, and other past times? Nope! I prefer listening to the Beatles, while Cindy enjoys the latest hits from *Diljit Dosanjh*. I could eat beans on toast seven days a week, but she would happily consume *Punjabi* food sat at the same table. Our path and pace towards spirituality initially differed, but that is okay because we were allowed to have individual differences. We have grown to realize that like the gears of a mechanical device, synchronicity is also important for optimal performance.

May everyone be blessed with a life partner who is their best friend, who is so content within their own shell that they can build a family structure that touches the blue sky above. One whose commitment to family and relationship is second to none; who fulfills all obligations to both those that are close to her and those that make up her village.

On the 26th of January 1994, I began to write a selection of letters to Cindy. Sometimes one a day, other times, two or three. This collection of letters ended on 28th April 1994, which was exactly two days before we were married. Over 160 pages of emotions, feelings, and desires for the future were openly shared with the person that was about to become my life partner. I knew then that I was being blessed…I continue to be blessed to this day!

Illustration by Nipun D Kasote

Randomness:

FAVOURITE MOVIES & SHOWS (IN NO PARTICULAR ORDER):

I think the score that supports a movie is as powerful as the moving images one sees on the screen, but this 'random' snippet isn't about music, but about movies. Now, my list could have been several pages, and to be honest, I could have written a chapter on the importance of film to my creative being. I think Star Wars (Episode IV: A New Hope (1977) and Star Trek: The Motion Picture (1979) both play a huge part in why I am a designer (and also the launch of shuttle Columbia on the 12th April 1981, an event I watched with Mr. Richardson, and a few other teachers, in the staff room) of my Primary School. Once I had understood that everything in those films were conceptualized and dreamt up by somebody, I wanted to do that too. But movies have done more than influence my career. It has emotionally moved me. I don't venture too far into the ocean/seas (Jaws), I am for the underdog (Braveheart, Gladiator, and *Shaheed*), I love the magical creativity of the Wizard of Oz and the humour around a sad chapter in our recent history of discrimination (Inglorious Bastards). I am sure some of these movies and TV shows will be on your list too...enjoy!

Shaheed (1965) - Grease – Jaws – Roots – Star Trek (1979) - *Sholay* – The Wizard of Oz - The Great Escape - Chitty Chitty Bang Bang - Mother India – The Exorcist – Evil Dead - *Suhaag* (1979) - Godfather I & II – Goodfellas – Forrest Gump - Schindler's List – Gladiator - Braveheart - Seven - Silence of the Lambs – Rocky I, II, III – Terminator - Saving Private Ryan - Inglorious Bastards – Ferris Bueller's Day Off - Crouching Tiger, Hidden Dragon - *Lagaan* – 3 Idiots - *Kabi Khushi Kabhie Gham* - *Gadar: Ek Prem Katha* - *Dilwale Dulhanhia Le Janyenga* - Taxi Driver - Apocalypto - The Lord of the Rings: The Fellowship of the Ring, The Two Towers, Return of the King - Raiders of the Lost Ark - Pan's Labyrinth - Chariots of Fire - Alien - Toy Story - *Dil Chahta Hai* (2001) Star Wars: Episode IV, A New Hope - The Elephant Man - Jesus of Nazareth - The King's Speech - Boyz n the Hood - Avatar - Monty Python and the Holy Grail - Dawn of the Dead - Malcolm X – Superman (1978) - The Lion King - The Dark Knight - *Rabb Da Radio* - *Angrej* (2015) – *Sajjan Singh Rangroot* - Game of Thrones

Illustration: The Godfather

Illustration 13: The Fake Fakir (2006)
by Kulbir Colin Singh Dhillon

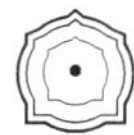

CHAPTER 9
Fake Fakir: Thank you

A few short years after our marriage, Cindy and I found ourselves on a quest for spirituality. This wasn't necessarily a joint decision, rather I was at the forefront pushing to be on a spiritual path, picking up from where I had left off before arriving in Canada.

In chapter 4, *Man of God*, I shared the initial kindling of my awakening towards something larger than myself. This journey was and continued to be cloaked by the label known as religion. I grew up going to a *Gurdwara* and doing both *seva* and singing religious hyms (*kirtan*) while being schooled on faith by my parents, and seniors at the *Gurdwara*. I continued to feel connected to something deep inside, but I lacked the knowledge to define what it was. What did emerge through my late teen years was an understanding that not everybody felt the same way, as naive as that may sound. What does it mean to feel empathy towards nature and humanity, to feel connected to ALL people, and not just your so-called own? To know that certain religious practices and rituals are inoperable. For the young and somewhat narrow scoped individual, the path and journey must be through the doors of a religious establishment and its doctrine.

The early 1990s were spent in the beautiful village of Bournville as an art student, and then up north to the City that reflects the attitudes and personality of a village; Sheffield. This was my home for three years, a time when children become young adults. My time was no different, I was blessed to experience the ups and downs of student life. I never tasted alcohol, though the odd doner kebab might have found its home deep in my tummy (I was a vegetarian for the most part!). My unshorn hair and a neatly tied turban allowed me to be recognized as a *Sikh*. I managed to juggle all aspects of student life and feel okay; not good or great, just okay! The inner turmoil, the challenges of academic life, and I guess the realization of my outlook on life which was quite different in many ways from how my parents might have perceived it, made life, just okay.

I arrive in Canada with my essential items which included several cassettes. CDs were available but cassette players were still the most common device used in vehicles, and on personal playing devices like the Sony Walkman! Three of these cassettes were given as a gift to Cindy when we first met. One was Simon and Garfunkel's, 'Bridge Over Troubled Water,' album. The soundtrack to the Bollywood movie, *Kabhi Kabhi*, and the last one was religious hymns sung by *Bhai Harjinder Singh Siri Nagar Wale!* I know, who does that? I did! I could recall what was said when these cassettes were being handed over, "These three albums will provide you with the essence of who I am." All three albums, their songs, and the lyrics can be classified as deep and with meaning – touching the soul and taking me on a journey.

My arrival in Canada was bittersweet. I had arrived in paradise but also knowing that my maternal uncle (*Mama Ji*), only had months to live. As devastating as that news was to me and as I completed my finals at university, I wanted to spend time with him.

I had a Compact Disc (CD) containing our *Sikh* scriptures, *Sri Guru Granth Sahib*, the eleventh *Guru* of the *Sikhs*, translated into the English language. I remember visiting Ontario *Khalsa Darbar* in November 1993 with my *Mama Ji.* There, we met with the President of the *Gurdwara* so that I could propose my idea of using the CD to project the scriptures onto screens placed in the main congregation hall, so that individuals such as myself, who didn't understand *Gurmukhi/Punjabi* language, could follow along with the singing of hymns and sermons in English and read the translations. I was told that my childish idea was against the *Sikh* code of conduct and disrespectful. He pointed to the cot on which the scriptures are usually placed and said, "That is the *Guru*, not this", tapping the case holding the set of CDs. Then, we left.

I attended the odd Saturday morning sermon at the local *Radha Soami* (Sect of *Sikhism*) gathering. Though a sect of the *Sikh* faith, many on both sides would beg to differ. They read and translate the *Sikh* scripture in both simple *Punjabi* and English! This was refreshing, though sitting on chairs instead of the floor did feel somewhat awkward. Nevertheless, I felt my time listening and understanding the words of the *Guru*, most rewarding on a spiritual level. My longing began to grow, I began to visualize my path in life, identify what gave me the most pleasure, and peace of mind. But this sect/cult was too narrow and not for me and Cindy. This was one of those topics that brought many a heated discussion; the outcome was an agreement to find a path that both of us felt we belonged to.

My next spiritual journey was taken with Cindy and my maternal auntie (*Mami Ji*), *Satpal Kaur Randhawa.* After the passing of *Mama Ji,* my *Mami Ji* was also on her own journey; a passage of personal growth that is rare in that generation of *Punjabi Sikhs*. Our search led us to Andrew Cohen, a New York-born spiritual teacher. After attending sessions in the Toronto area, we decided to attend his two-day retreat in Boston, Massachusetts. The retreat was focused on hours of meditation with extremely bland vegetarian food to look forward to. Though Andrew has had some challenges, it must be said that his explanation and techniques around meditation have continued to be useful.

All of these experiences felt foreign; their practises and culture just didn't sit well with us both. Then, we decided to explore opportunities with our faith: *Sikhism.* Our scriptures are globally recognized to share a universal message of love. They ask the reader to go on the inner journey in order for him or her to understand the meaning of life. Together, we became newly baptized *Sikhs* and were guided by a holy man; a spiritual teacher we met at *Singh Sabha Gurdwara* in Malton, Ontario, in May 1996. I was clean-shaven and without my turban, as I had been for just over two years. Not much had changed personally beyond my outer appearance. I remember standing in front of the mirror and running the razor blade across my jawline on that particular Sunday, which was two days before taking the *Sikh* ceremony of initiation (*Amrit Sanchar)* from this spiritual teacher.

His sermons were passionate and emotionally fierce. He brought our rich Saint Soldier history to life, created a want to be part of, and belong to a powerful yet unknown force some of us called *God.*

He became so integral to our lives. Not only did we introduce him to our families, but we also travelled to India on spiritual retreats led by him for over the next eight years.

We were so intent on satisfying the hunger in our minds, on learning as much as we could from this man that we did not realize our naivety had taken over and our judgement was clouded. We were following a fake, a snake-oil salesman, and a completely phony *fakir* (*Fakir*; [fuh-keer] an ascetic, member of a religious order). It was not until a fellow devotee approached us and shared that she had been allegedly sexually assaulted by this man, who we all trusted. She was distraught, and it was obvious what she said was true. Our journey to enlightenment and spirituality came to a crashing halt. Was she in fact telling the truth? How did we know she was telling the truth? But why would she lie about something like this? We had been following this "so-called" holy man for eight years, why didn't we see this coming? There were so many questions, but no answers! This was not an accusation that we could let slide, it was very serious. The essence of *Sikhism* is to stand up for those that are oppressed and fight for their rights. We reflected on the past eight years of our lives; were there questionable moments that we experienced when we were in the presence of this "holy man"... it was then that we started our personal investigation. We delved further and were horrified to learn that this so-called holy man has had sexual relationships with young women for decades.

Our next journey; justice for his victims, took years of hard work and perseverance. Our goal was to end his holy facade and topple him from his throne of deceit.

From a young age, I always asked the question why did the likes of Jesus, Moses, *Buddha*, *Krishna*, our *Sikh Gurus* and the rest of the band of merry men, come before my time on this planet? I am here NOW, yet these great souls came centuries ago. Why not now? Is it not always better to be given the sermon directly from the teacher? Would the impact not be greater on one's life to feel the passion directly from the teacher, his/her energy first-hand, rather than word-of-mouth or through the teachings narrated or captured on paper?

The usual response my father would give is "Great souls are always walking the earth." Really? The likes of Jesus, *Buddha*, or *Guru Nanak* are around, even today. Saying such is deemed blasphemous, but why? Why did the sons, daughters, and prophets of God all appear generations, millennia before those of us reading this book? Does this make sense? Who decides who will succeed in becoming worshiped by millions, versus being a relatively unknown entity, a small-time philosopher or teacher? Let's not be naïve here. Some great religions of our time have been spread by the sword, rather than the verses of love and compassion. Don't drink all the Kool-Aid...keep an open mind!

I have always been a searcher, feeling the pull from within and looking for answers. This is not because I did not have anything better to do. Trust me, I did, and I still do, but I always felt there was something more than just being born, living, and then dying. Did I believe in life after death? Yes, absolutely! Did I theorize about some Judeo-Christian visual of heaven and hell? Of course, most *Sikhs* had been led to assume a realm that we all go to, a place called Heaven (*Sachkand*) or Hell *(Narak)*. This religious doctrine's influence occurred at the time of the British rule of India when a massive effort to *Anglicise* the Indian people and their culture and faiths was undertaken (1878-1947). Mass conversions and the injection of Christian religious practises and the mistranslation of sacred scriptures and beliefs left a lasting mark, something the *Sikh* faith is still wrestling with even today!

My home, social, cultural, and religious upbringing had answers, just like all our backgrounds do. The general flow of this section of questions and answers usually came with, "We are on this earth to do good, and to follow God's word". Then, depending on your behaviour pattern, and the score you accumulated in the *game of life*, you either go UP to heaven and chill with the dude we call God, or you end up south, DOWN in Hell. I was a drinker of the Kool-Aid just as most people are. Parents and teachers would consistently instill this into us, it became gospel and so we follow along, like sheep. I grazed these meadows for many years, when I was younger, I even travelled across other pastures, with the permission of my parents, and attended Sunday school with my English friends. Why? Because I had always heard/felt a calling…

In 1996, we began to hear stories about a holy man (*Sant/Fakir*) from India. According to Wikipedia, A *Sant* is someone who has knowledge of self, truth, reality and is revered by others. This holy man was said to be baptizing hundreds, if not thousands into the *Sikh* fold. His disciples talked about his powerful sermons, which would not only recap our history but shared the great stories of our *Gurus* and the great *Sikhs* who followed the path of righteousness and enlightenment.

Some could argue, decades and centuries had elapsed since the community had apparently witnessed such a powerful character. They said his passion would move even the most non-believers among us to the point that they would call themselves reborn. He was scheduled to arrive in the Toronto area in May 1996. The *Gurdwara* was absolutely full to the rafters. It was a sea of colours and the air was thick with anticipation, and the curiosity of thousands wanting to have a glimpse of this holy man. As we walked in and paid homage to our *Guru* (the *Sikh* Scriptures), I looked over to the right and saw that I could squeeze into a spot up front on the floor, as we all sit on the floor in the *Gurdwara*, and kindly thank my brothers around me for allowing me to squeeze in. But I had to be right up at the front. I wanted to bear witness to this great soul I had heard so many stories about.

Pseudo-Sant (is how we will address this individual/holy man/ Sant/Fakir) was a holy man that came from *Haryana*, India. He travelled the world preaching the teachings of the Sikh *Gurus* through his music and motivational speaking. He would recite scriptures and tell stories of the lives of the *Sikh Gurus*, and sing hymns that contained 'extracts' of the *Sikh* scriptures. His entourage on stage included other musicians and gentlemen that could sit and look spiritual. The language he spoke in was every-day-*Punjabi*. It was what we were used to hearing, very common to the ears. Though the Scriptures are written in *Punjabi* (*Gurmukhi* being the correct term). Like all languages, it becomes old and difficult to understand because we today do not use those words (a bit like Shakespearean English!)

As he walked into the hall, this large man had a fierce and powerful look about him. He was dressed in white from turban to his long flowing tunic and a white scarf around his neck. He made his way onto the stage and began to play a tune on the *harmonium* (pump organ). The melody was enchanting. For those of you that listen to top quality music, you might be familiar with The Who's song, *Baba O'Riley* (named after Peter Townsend's philosophical and musical influences, Meher Baba and Terry Riley). That melody at the beginning must have its roots in the East. Truth be told, there is nothing quite like this musical portion of a sermon when it connects with you internally with the energy source. It transcends the physical realm, if you allow it to, and takes you through a journey of internal bliss, changing your mindset; your current emotional state, like a damp, warm cloth cleaning a black slate board.

His voice was loud, full of confidence, and authority. When he spoke, you had no choice but to listen and become interested and engaged. His passionate words, his storytelling can only be described today as an OLED 4K large screen; the image being described was just short of being in 3D or eXtended reality. It was something I had never experienced before, and judging by thousands in the large hall, it was something like being at the opening night to a much-anticipated movie, with the audience being predominantly comprised of fans. I was fully engaged with his stories. His words were descriptive, his voice would elevate your emotions, the storyline was being depicted as if it was taking place right in front of your very eyes. Undoubtedly, his passion during his performance was electrifying. Who. Was. This. Man?

After finishing his sermon, it is common practice for people like *Pseudo-Sant*, who are considered to be holy, to be invited into the homes of members of the congregation to bless their homes. Let me provide you with a glimpse; a taste of how it looked and felt. Sheep were flocking to their shepherd, everybody was in a jovial mood, lots of pearly white teeth, and a sprinkling of excitement could be sensed. You were about to be in the presence of a great soul, an enlightened being. What topic were his 'up-close' personal sermons going to be about? Would he detect the *real* you and call you out for it? I am sure it did not look much different than a scene from Franco Zeffirelli's 1977 epic, *Jesus of Nazareth*, when Jesus went to the house of Peter the fisherman of Galilee, and poor Peter was trying to stop his humble abode from crumbling under the strains of human inquisitiveness. There was not a large following of first or second-generation Canadian or *Sikhs* born in the West. The clear majority were immigrants from *Punjab*, India. The fact that I was clean-shaven at this stage in my life also added to the heightened interest we were both generating. At one point, we got to sit down with *Pseudo-Sant* and talk on a personal level. It was daunting, but rewarding too. I simply had one ask:

"Give me that jewel within that lessens my wants and desires in life"

"Deh Naam Santokhia, utre man ki bukh"

– Guru Granth Sahib, page 958

It was a line from the *Sikh* scriptures that had touched me a few years back. If I could lessen the wants in life, be them materialistic or desires of other kinds, then I was possibly heading towards an aspect of spirituality. The roadblocks in my life's journey should be fewer, right? He absolutely loved the fact that this was my wish. I was not looking for a blessing to get a job, a house, get married, have a child, money, and so on.

No, here was a young man at the age of twenty-five asking for guidance, wanting to run the opposite way from the masses. Though time with him was limited, his entourage would do his work, they were the closers. The PR campaign was impressive, so much so that only days after meeting this *Fakir*, both Cindy and I decided to become baptized *Sikhs* and start our true inner journey.

From 1996 to 2003, seven and a half years of our lives were dedicated to this holy man, and through him, to the *Sikh* faith as we understood it. He would claim to treat both of us as his children (*Pseudo-Sant* was a *Sikh* monk. He and others like him did not get married. When asked why, they said that they were devoted to one love, and that was the *Sikh* scriptures; the 11th *Guru* of the *Sikhs*). We travelled extensively all around the globe with him, helping to support his mission and spread the *Sikh* faith within our own community (We *Sikhs* are not big on converting, actually we do not convert for the most part. If you like our way of life, our religious garb and message, welcome onboard).

Without us realizing it, we were both a part of his global PR campaign. Some would say that outside of his entourage, we were possibly the closest to him. Whenever we went to India, to his *Ashram* (*Dera*), we would be provided accommodation in his exclusive area, and with no limitations to gaining access to him. "You are both my children. We have been together in many past lives too. One day, I will explain to you both who you are…" these words alone would act like a drug, providing stamina and support for living a high-paced, gruelling lifestyle, especially when we were with him (our routine usually consisted of going to sleep at 2am after bathing, reciting the scriptures and meditating, only to be awoken at 7:00am as we prepared to attend the multiple events throughout India. The pace was so gruelling I usually would end up getting sick from being physically worn out). With Cindy being born in Canada, and me being born in England, and choosing to follow the path of *Sikhism*, we became examples he wanted to share across the stages he performed on. He would ask us to join him on stage where some of the events attracted tens of thousands of individuals. The venues were the historic *Sikh Gurdwara's* throughout India and then all the major cities in Europe and North America. We were both humbled and proud to be chosen to support this mission. We were in the heart of a historic event... little did we know we would be in the eye of a storm.

Everything in our lives was about him and the *Sikh* faith. I personally helped to establish two classes at the largest *Sikh Gurdwaras* in Southern Ontario. Within months of starting the class, the attendance at Ontario *Khalsa Darbar* grew to over 200 children. I also hosted a TV show called *Insight into Sikhism* which aired every Saturday evening. These were the years in which we felt a lot of communal love and oneness of congregation (*Sangat*).

I had always delved into the art of meditation and for the most part, it can be described as, "licking a rock and expecting to extract a flavour". I enjoyed the learning process. The science of going within, to search for oneself, and for the cosmic energy we call God. Most *Sikhs* are told they need a guide, a teacher on the inner journey. Meeting *Pseudo-Sant* seemed to be my destiny. I was asking for *answers*, to know more. He appeared like *Mr. Ben* (a British cartoon character from the late 1970s and early 1980s, who always appeared dressed in the right outfit to assist).

One's mind can be described as a memory storage device connected to a slideshow of one's life events. It only takes a millisecond for the emotions to engage that memory bank and for those images, normally of the moving-picture kind, to materialize. There are many experiences that stood out. In the summer of 1996, as we were being driven to the *Gurdwara* in Yuba City, California, he turned his head around slightly, looking towards the rear seats with his peripheral vision, from the passenger seat and said to Cindy and me, "If you forget to do your daily prayers I can forgive you. If you fall back on your meditation schedule and lose track of a few days here and there, that too I can forgive, but children, if you ever let your character be tarnished, I can never forgive that. Understood?" "Yes", we replied. He then pointed towards his white turban and said, "Never let a black stain appear on my white turban, children." I remember the happiness that oozed from within and around us. We didn't have to talk about what was just said. No, it was gospel passages to our ears. Within days of meeting him, *Pseudo-Sant* confirmed in one swoop of a sentence the significance of character. It was the most important aspect of one's personality traits. We both felt it was the foundation upon which you build,

You. Little did we know then that in less than eight years, his character would change the course of many lives.

Depeche Mode's, *Personal Jesus* seemed an appropriate title for those years with the *Pseudo-Sant*. People had to pray and ask God for direction, and then hope to hear, feel or get a response. Not us! We simply asked his embodiment, his representative on earth. All major decisions in our life were first discussed with him. We had what is called blind faith, which entails that we follow without ever questioning and giving ourselves completely. The stories and fables in *Sikhism* and all other religions supported blind faith. Those that lived by these tenets were on the receiving end of God's blessings. The congregation was like a support network. When you were not engaged directly with the *Pseudo-Sant*, you spent time with your brothers and sisters (this is how we addressed one another). You could relax and talk about worldly things, but a good childhood story of *Pseudo-Sant* doing something wonderful was always only a few sentences away. We all ate from the same steel dishes; we created bonds of friendship with many.

Over the course of our time with him, many members of the congregation would come and go. People that seemed integral to the inner community, what we call key individuals. We would turn up in India to find that they were no longer there. Why/how? It would emotionally bruise you. The spiritual loss of loved ones was always troubling to an extent and the stories surrounding their departure, for the most part, always seemed to be steeped in negativity. Did anyone ever leave and did not get maligned in some shape or form by the inner circle and directly by *Pseudo-Sant*? As our years of service grew, so did the number of stories. Something was not right.

In November of 2003, we were informed by the victim herself of what had transpired. This event would change the course of our lives…

Pseudo-Sant had allegedly sexually assaulted and raped a member of his congregation. The account of the ordeal and its details, as they were being shared were as clear as if we had witnessed them ourselves. He was more than a teacher/guide to us both. He meant the world to us...but not beyond the boundaries of character!

We delicately questioned some members of his *Ashrams*. The ones that we built close relationships with, and who ever we talked to put their heads down in shame, and said, "Now, you know why members of the congregation leave suddenly. They too have heard about his wrong-doings and simply walk away into the shadows. This is not the first victim. This has been going on for over a decade". They shared the details of some of the horror stories. Stories of sex slaves; women that were kept in his *ashram* for his pleasures and then provided financial support to live out their lives within the *ashram* as cooks and cleaners. He was careful when choosing his victims. They would normally be from very poor families, a house that had many girls. He would offer to pay for the victim's sisters' dowry and weddings, as part of the deal for them to keep their mouths tightly shut. This time he chose the wrong victim.

Do you think you can refrain from sexual desires? How many horror stories have we heard, globally of priests from all denominations taking advantage of young boys or girls? It is an absurd thing to think you do not need to have a healthy sexual relationship with a loved one. Those desires will not be crushed. Those natural tendencies that are part of the evolution are not going to stop my friends. The *Sikh Gurus* made it clear that we should all live a married life. Try and have children and in the process, fulfill your sexual desires with your loved one. Yet, these fake *fakirs*, these charlatans, men in the guise of a holy man, choose to refrain from being married, instead take advantage of innocent souls.

Several months after the events became public, one of my ex-students from one of the classes I had helped to establish, wrote a blog about this whole ordeal. He compared my situation with Malcolm X's, referencing this young passionate leader's realization that his own spiritual teacher, his beloved *Elijah Muhammed*, was fathering children out of wedlock. It shook the very core of Malcolm's existence. My student went on to say that there was a time when I would have taken a bullet for *Pseudo-Sant*. The debate was fermenting within the community about the shocking scandal. I began to sympathize with those that face such traumatic events in their own lives. Your initial thoughts are to keep something like this covered up, away from the eyes and ears of the world. It is painful and emotionally draining to be within and around such a scandal. Being a protectionist about such situations does make emotional sense. Rather than airing dirty laundry in public and stopping the rot from setting in, to cover it up without doing root cause remedies. The fact remains *Pseudo-Sant* was a rapist and a fake *fakir*, and if we were accusing him of such heinous crimes with written statements by the victims, then everybody in the community needed to listen, as they should have done to Brother Malcolm. My young student was not too far from the truth. Yes, I probably would have taken a bullet for *Pseudo-Sant*.

Over the next few years, from 2003 to 2007, I spent hundreds of hours and a lot of my free time trying to get justice for the victim and to bring him to justice, both within the faith and by preventing him from preaching globally.

Pseudo-Sant was a very powerful man in India. He had friends that were in all levels of government and connections within the police forces. Just like we had respected him, hundreds and thousands of others did too. This David had to take on that Goliath, just as *Krishna* took on his uncle, the tyrant ruler *Kansa*. The uphill battle had begun. As my parents reminded me, 'our beloved 10th *Guru* asks us to stand for what is right, no matter the personal cost'.

Over the next few years, I was contacting all levels of authorities both in Canada and the United States of America, the FBI, and CSIS. We had a legal document, sworn statements, and all we wanted was to revoke his visa to prevent him from preaching outside of India. I was talking to individuals that have been involved with government agencies and the stories that unfolded were shocking. This *Pseudo-Sant* had deep roots within agencies in India.

I received death threats on my home phone. Threats being made towards me, my wife, and children, telling me to shut up and back off, or else...The calls were coming from all over, the UK, US, and Canada., from people that obviously knew more than we did and felt the need to keep it covered up. I purchased recording equipment and began to collect evidence. These threats only stopped when the local police authorities got involved and contacted the instigators directly.

India was out of bounds for several years. He was that connected and had friends in high places that we knew he could have paid the legal authorities to take unjust action against us. What would have happened next could have been even more dangerous, but at no point did I feel that I should stop supporting the cause.

It was not just the experience of being hurt by your beloved spiritual teacher that made me question the pedestal upon which we place others. Yes, hindsight is 20/20, and many people have lined up and said, "You should follow and believe in only the teachings of the *Sikh* Scriptures, and not a living Teacher/*Guru*/*Sant*/*Fakir*".

It was not the day-to-day battles that made me reassess my religious and spiritual life. I was also fortunate or unfortunate, depending upon your viewpoint, to have an audience with the

Jathedar (so-called leader of the *Sikh* Community/Nation) of the *Sikhs* holiest Shrine, *Harmandir Sahib (Golden Temple)*, *Amritsar*, *Punjab*. I explained the details of what had unfolded. His reaction to this horrific set of events was somewhat numb. He said he would address the concerns presented, which included sworn statements by the victim. As I finished stating the facts about the fake *fakir*, the *Jathedar* of the *Sikh's* second holiest shrine, *Anandpur Sahib*, *Punjab* opened up and shared that he already knew the 'real' story, which was based upon lies they had already been fed. This led me to challenge these so-called leaders of their faith and describe the papacy/establishment (*Akal Takht*) as an empty vessel (a hollow-sounding container filled with nothing but hot air). Voices were raised on all sides, swords were nearly drawn, and I was asked to leave. I refused. The fight continued, even though the corrupt leaders refused to provide support.

After many years of fighting a never-ending feud, it was time to move ahead. We won many of the battles and maybe even the war, but the level of corruption and illegal tactics being used by this man had no end. I have been brought up in nations and societies that taught me to fight with some level of ethics and morals. The guerilla warfare lasted close to four years. I was able to mobilize supporters in multiple continents, fighting on multiple fronts with the end result being a generational change of attitude towards these *Pseudo-Sants*; fake *fakirs*. This chapter in my life needed closure.

The title of this chapter must include the words 'thank you'. If it was not for these most valuable life lessons, if it was not for the eight years of following a so-called spiritual teacher and then another four years working tirelessly to end his global reign, I might have carried on, relying upon another instead of doing the hard work myself. Toppling this *Pseudo-Sants* was like a domino effect. That period in the mid-1990s read like a laundry list of wannabe holy men, fake *fakirs* catching flights out of India to the lands of milk and honey (let us not forget the value of the Indian rupee versus the pound sterling or the US/Canadian dollar; it paid to preach in the West!). Our *seva* put a stop to many *Pseudo-Sants*...but people usually learn the hard way, no?

Life's journey throws curve balls at us all the time. It is how you maneuver and react to those balls that define the outcome of your life's game. After living through this decade-long ordeal, some might feel it to be the worst situation of their lives. Some might describe that decade as the missing days, months, and years of one's life that you can never retrieve. Instead, how about the most valuable lesson provided by being a part of this experience? One of the biggest questions of our existence is, "What are we here for? What happens to us when we die, and what should we do to live a good life?" As mentioned earlier, my own personal journey was one of self-realization and a true want to lessen the desire for material things. This fact that my own personal relationship with my so-called creator is now stronger and I feel at peace rather than feeling lost due to past experiences. I decided to undertake my own learning using the *Guru Granth Sahib* as my reference point. As mentioned earlier, those that have read the scriptures talk about the beautiful poetic verse, promoting the oneness of humanity, and the message of merging with the creator as you live in this material world. I have continued to do selfless service, but I do not feel it needs to be done strictly at a house of worship. It can be and should be done where one sees a need and understands that he or she can provide support. This willingness to help others is the foundation of all faiths. Rather, I should say, it is the foundation of humanity, which is the greatest of faiths.

Let me start with Luke 17:21…'the kingdom of God is within you'. *Guru Nanak* also clarified that God is the eternal being (*Akal Murat*), and the formless one (*Nirankar*), and un-incarnated (*Ajuni*) and self-existent (*Saibhang*). It simply is…timeless, boundless, formless, ever-existent, immutable, and ineffable. My God is energy. My personal search for life's answer truly began after my time with the *Pseudo-Sant.* My personal journey continues, and I can say that I live a blessed life. My eyes have been open and my heart has been touched and the energy within this vehicle will forever be free, forever be in love, forever be…

The chapter barely scratches the surface of the eight-year ordeal. It has been a decisive chapter in my life. The emotional highs and lows at the time were truly insurmountable. It affected every cell, organ, and tissue, my energy and aura both in and around my body. Only God knows the emotional trauma and rebirth of mind and outlook that was achieved because of this episode. My glass is always half-full!

CHAPTER 10
MY FAITH

*"In 1469, Guru Nanak was born in Punjab, India.
His message of equality and peace under one formless energy source (God) was a revolt against religious doctrines, cultural stigmas, and tyranny.
His revelation was implemented not by the sword but through the poetic verses he wrote and sung.
Guru Nanak's simple message of direct communion, with a non-judgmental universal creative force, acted as a catalyst to challenge the status quo of existing beliefs. Let's not accept things blindly in the name of tradition, but rather challenge the spiritual blemishes and soulless doctrines that have begun to plague our faith. Set aflame that revolutionary fire burn from deep within and set stagnation and dogma a light.
My Guru(s) were revolutionaries; why am I expected to be a sheep?"*

- By Kulbir Colin Singh Dhillon (2012)

I am a *Sikh*, and my faith has a pluralistic view of the world. Our guide is our eleventh *guru*, the *Guru Granth Sahib*, (the sacred scriptures of the *Sikh* religion). The inclusion of people is integral to our faith's culture. The Holy Scriptures not only contain the teachings of six of the ten *Sikh Gurus* but also Hindu and Muslim saints/mystics too! The first *Guru, Guru Nanak's* message inspires and reinvigorates all those who chose to listen. India is an old wise land with spirituality flowing through its rivers and impregnating its soil. It is human nature to search deep for the meaning of life. We followed religions rich in mythology, created deities as character templates to guide our behaviours and to address the worry of life after death. *Guru Nanak's* philosophy was more immediate. We are not monotheism, but rather a monism faith. We believe in the oneness of the universe versus one God. Also, we strongly believe that an individual is responsible and accountable for his or her shortcomings/ gains. *Sikhism* has some basic principles; there are the physical representations of the faith, such as the turban, beard, the steel bangle (*Kara*), and a ceremonial dagger carried on a black strap across one's chest (*Kirpan*), to name but a few. Then, there are three guiding tenants asked of all members of the faith;

1. ***Kirt Karna*** - *Earn an honest living*
2. ***Vand ke Chhakna*** - *Share with others*
3. ***Naam Japna*** - *Meditate (connecting with yourself and the cosmic energy)*

These three are the foundational stones of not only the *Sikh* faith but by any individual from any religion or denomination who practices it, which is the essence of a beautiful life journey. It entails earning an honest living, which you then share with those in need while you pay homage to the energy force within. It is a life with minimal vices but full of virtues, where you grow as an individual, understanding that your thoughts and actions can influence your immediate and distant environment. Utopia? Maybe, but whether you are worried about your own ecosystem or the world, this message is universal. It emphasizes *Sikhism's* place in this world. Part of the journey of a *Sikh*, possibly the most essential aspect, involves going on the internal pilgrimage. It is that journey to meet the real you and to begin communication with your maker. There are obstacles along the way, akin to roadblocks in our daily lives. *Sikhism* broke it down to humans having five drivers that could influence our actions. Anything in excess is just not healthy, not to say they are evil or wicked; they can be seen as drivers of the chariot, which is our human body. They do not have to control the speed or the direction in which that temporal vehicle goes. However, our higher consciousness dictates how much power each is given, so that we are always in control of them, instead of having them drive us.

***The FIVE Vices**

Kaam | Lust
Krodh | Anger
Lobh | Greed
Moh | Attachment
Hankaar | Ego

---

*The vices and virtues described in the Sikh faith are also recognized by the Hindus, Buddhists, and Jains; the religions of the Indian Sub-Continent.

Like tidal waves or *tsunamis* that overwhelm everything in their midst, people will take pure words of a philosophy they have adopted and manipulate them to support his/her motives. Those ulterior motives are usually powered by the lack of control over the five drivers?. So, how do we overcome, or at least try to conquer these drivers?

The mind has to be conquered or controlled. It's the root of all things in our lives. The mind creates every situation and circumstance in your life, and without putting it to a task or without stopping to ask its motive, the results can be socially/ economically/culturally disastrous. Challenge yourself and question the purpose of your actions. Before you can progress mentally or spiritually, you must start the pilgrimage within. You must go deep inside and reflect. Meditation and quiet time are tools that can be called upon to decide how much free reign you can give the drivers. Before I even attempt to understand someone else, I have to first understand myself. How do you accomplish this? You begin by being truthful to yourself. Be critical of yourself and map out your positive and/or negative attributes. Then, see how you may be able to change some of the negative aspects embedded deep within you.

"Know thyself"

(Ancient Greek Aphorism) - Plato

You will be surprised at how many of these character blemishes are avoidable, by tweaking the amount of control we give over to the vices. Take Anger. Unchecked anger can destroy relationships and careers, not to mention the unseen harm it can do to the physical body. It is also capable of consuming us alive from within. When we get to this point, know that the vices are what drive us. But you can take some of the anger and use it as fuel to propel a positive change. Anger, as an emotion, itself is not bad. Without it, there would be no justice. Anger assisted in stopping the slave trade. Anger supported women's right to vote. Without anger to fuel those movements, the march to societal progression would have been much slower in a similar mode, without the emotion of Lust, healthy relationships where love and respect are strong can dwindle. Without some sprinkling of Greed, one could be less resourceful and possibly lacking in the means to drive innovations. Like anything else in this world, you can learn/unlearn a lot of your personality traits. It just requires time and immense effort. Holy people, people of the cloth, those who decide to spend their lives in the service of a higher power, are in essence trying to find themselves. They endeavour to become one with the cosmic energy source, known as God, and control the five vices, within themselves. This is the journey to enlightenment.

You might go through life thinking that this is the be-all and end-all, but it's not. Even if you don't prescribe to the philosophy of reincarnation or after-life, the principle to use this energy to propel ourselves to a better state is still universal. Most people need to adopt a faith or to follow a religion to find that consciousness, but that is not always necessary. We can improve ourselves and aim to live this life in complete harmony with whatever we perceive to be kind, real, and positive. What prevents us from doing so is our Ego.

"When I am in my ego, then you are not with me. Now that you are with me, there is no egotism within me. The wind may raise up huge waves in the vast ocean, but they are just water in water."

"jab ham hote tab too naahee ab toohee mai naahee,
anal agam jaise lahar mi odhadh jal keval jal maa(n)hee."

– Guru Granth Sahib, page 657

Getting to know oneself, shrinking ego, or controlling one's ego are all taken care of when you begin to understand your true self. Quiet time and daily self-reflection can assist with checking in on ourselves and diminishing the effects of ego. From the early 90s to the mid-2000s, I spent time meditating, pretty much on a daily basis. There are many techniques to going on the inner pilgrimage. Some talk about focusing on a particular mantra, others talk about letting your thoughts come and go to simply acknowledge them, but not to focus on them. Some ask you to be silent; to silence the mind. Part of the meditation/quiet time tool-chest is breathing; techniques to assist with focusing and calming your inner environment and allowing you to know yourself even more. All of these are supportive in controlling the egotistical nature of humans if only to fact-check the right/wrongs within yourself!

"Knowing others is wisdom; knowing yourself is Enlightenment. He who knows others is wise; He who know himself is Enlightened."

- Lao Tzu

Serving humanity can also help to eliminate ego and lead you on a path of enlightenment. What is this word "enlightenment", and what does it mean to me? For some, it seems to describe the final destiny of one's spiritual journey. It could be a destination they spend a lifetime trying to reach. For me, it's the realization of oneself. We have somehow managed to dull the bright light of one's true self; that energy source that is part of the cosmic energy source we call God. Removing the layers, cleaning your internal mirror, that realization and the understanding is enlightenment. One who is enlightened has only realized or found themselves. Going back to the assumption of a journey, you have just started the voyage. To be selfless is an integral part of the *Sikh* way of life. I started this by chapter talking about the founder of the *Sikh* faith, *Guru Nanak* born in 1469. Before he left his physical body, the responsibilities for continuing on with service to humanity fell upon *Guru Angad*, the second *Guru*. He was not a family member, but the *Guru's* most astute student who carried on and added to the work of the founder.

The 10th *Guru* of the *Sikhs, Guru Gobind Singh* was born in 1666: The year of the Great Fire of London. It was the same year Samuel Pepys reported on the world's first blood transfusion and the year that French King Luis XIV founded the French Academy of Sciences. I share these events and their dates to emphasize how relatively new the *Sikh* faith is, in context to some of the old religions. Timelines and contextual diagrams are a brilliant tool for placing things within a specific time in history.

Randomness:

SIKH GURUS ASCENSION TO GURUSHIP (WORLD EVENTS TIMELINE TABLE)

Sikh Gurus	Year of Guruship	World Events
1 Guru Nanak Dev Ji	1469	The War of the Roses between Richard Neville, 16th Earl of Warwick against Edward IV of England.
		Ferdinand II of Aragon marries Isabella I of Castile, a marriage that paves the way to the unification of Aragon and Crown of Castile into a single country, Spain.
2 Guru Angad Dev Ji	1539	Charles V, Holy Roman Emperor (and Charles I of Spain) and Francis I of France sign the Treaty of Toledo, agreeing to make no further alliances with England. The treaty comes after Henry VIII of England splits with Rome and Pope Paul III.
		Spain annexes Cuba.
		Jews of Tyrnau Hungary expelled. Spanish explorer Hernando de Soto discovers Florida.
		Lutheranism is forcibly introduced into Iceland, despite the opposition of Bishop Jon Arason.
		The first printing press in North America is set up in Mexico City.
3 Guru Amar Das Ji	1552	The first printing press in North America is set up in Mexico City.
		France signs secret treaty with German Protestants.
		Conquest of Kazan by Ivan the Terrible (Grozny).
		The Act of Uniformity imposes the Book of Protestant Common Prayer on England.

Sikh Gurus	Year of Guruship	World Events
		In Italy, Bartolomeo Eustachi completes his Tabulae anatomicae, presenting his discoveries on the structure of the inner ear and heart, although for fear of the Inquisition, it will not be published until 1714.
		King Edward VI of England founds 35 grammar schools by royal charter, including Shrewsbury; Leeds Grammar School.
4 Guru Ram Das Ji	1574	France begins 5th Holy War against Huguenots.
		Murad III succeeds Selim II as Ottoman Sultan.
		Henry III follows brother Charles IX as king of France.
		Manila, Philippines, gains cityhood.
5 Guru Arjun Dev Ji	1581	The Parliament of England's Act against Reconciliation to Rome imposes heavy fines, for practicing Catholicism.
		Francis Drake knighted by Queen Elizabeth I abroad Golden Hind at Deptford.
		A meteorite makes landfall in Thuringia, Holy Roman Empire (present-day Germany).
6 Guru Hargobind Ji	1606	England adopts the Union Flag, replaced in 1801 by current Union Flag/Union Jack.
		2,000 Foreigners murdered in Russia.
		Shakespeare's first possible performance of Macbeth, in Hampton Court for King James I.
		Virginia Company settlers leave London to establish Jamestown, Virginia.

Sikh Gurus	Year of Guruship	World Events
		The trial of Guy Fawkes and other conspirators, for plotting against Parliament and James I of England, begins.
7 Guru Angad Dev Ji	1644	Pilgrims in Boston report America's 1st UFO siting.
		200 members of Peking imperial family/court commit suicide in loyalty to the Emperor.
		Florentine scientist Evangelista Torricelli describes his invention of the mercury barometer.
		Plague breaks out in Edinburgh.
		Antonio Stradivari, Italian violin maker is born.
8 Guru Harkrishan Ji	1661	Oliver Cromwell is exhumed and subjected to a posthumous execution after having been dead for two years.
		King Charles II of England, Scotland and Ireland is crowned in Westminster Abbey for the second time.
		Isaac Newton admitted as a student to Trinity College, Cambridge.
		1st banknotes in Europe are issued by Bank of Stockholm.
		Battle of Kushliki: Polish-Lithuanian forces defeat the Russian army.
9 Guru Teg Bahadur Ji	1665	The Journal des scavans begins publication in France, the first scientific journal.
		Bucharest allows Jews to settle in the city, in exchange for an annual tax of 16 guilders.
		The Great Plague forces the closure of the University of Cambridge, where Isaac

Sikh Gurus	Year of Guruship	World Events
		In Italy, Bartolomeo Eustachi completes his Tabulae anatomicae, presenting his discoveries on the structure of the inner ear and heart, although for fear of the Inquisition, it will not be published until 1714.
		King Edward VI of England founds 35 grammar schools by royal charter, including Shrewsbury; Leeds Grammar School.
(10) Guru Gobind Singh Ji	1675	France begins 5th Holy War against Huguenots.
		Murad III succeeds Selim II as Ottoman Sultan.
		Henry III follows brother Charles IX as king of France.
		Manila, Philippines, gains cityhood.
(11) Guru Granth Sahib Ji	1708	England adopts the Union Flag, replaced in 1801 by current Union Flag/Union Jack.
		2,000 Foreigners murdered in Russia.
		Shakespeare's first possible performance of Macbeth, in Hampton Court for King James I.
		Virginia Company settlers leave London to establish Jamestown, Virginia.

World event details courtesy of
http://www.onthisday.com/ & http://en.wikipedia.org/wiki/[date]

The tenth *Guru* decided to end the human **Guru* concept and place the collective teachings called the *Adi Granth* as the 11th *Guru* of the *Sikhs*. The instructions were to help all those that choose to read and learn from them. The purpose was for anyone to be able to find a path to enlightenment, and personal freedom from the five vices, without the need for a physical teacher or intermediary. There was no requirement for anyone striving to attain the highest possible level of consciousness to detach oneself from the material world.

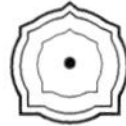

---

*Guru: The dispeller of darkness, the guide, teacher. The word originates from the ancient Sanskrit language but is prevalent in all Indian dialects and languages (that's over 120 languages and over 1,000 dialects.)

I have studied the scriptures of the great religions, but I do not find elsewhere the same power of appeal to the heart and mind as I find here in these volumes (Sri Guru Granth Sahib). They are compact in spite of their length and are a revelation of the concept of God to the recognition and indeed the insistence upon the practical needs of the human body. There is something strangely modern about these scriptures and this puzzled me until I learned that they are in fact comparatively modern, compiled as late as the 16th century when explorers were beginning to discover the globe upon which we all live is a single entity divided only by arbitrary lines of our making. Perhaps this sense of unity is the source of power I find in these volumes. They speak to a person of any religion or of none. They speak to the human heart and the searching mind."

- Miss Pearl S. Buck, Nobel Laureate

The philosophy of *Sikhism* is one of devotion and inward thinking. The ideology is wholly universal, and no group of people are deemed as the chosen ones! It celebrates the unique relationship between the individual and the supreme energy that brought that individual into being, no matter the name given to that energy by different people. The *Guru Granth Sahib* is not an interpretation of the words of the actual founders of the faith. However, it is the exact words written by them, so there is no room for ideas to be lost in translation as there has been for others.

My faith and identity have been a crucial part of my life. Daily, I represent my faith and the great teachers of the past. I stand out in a crowd and answer questions about who I am. I have had to assert my identity as a Sikh man. I have been challenged and attacked for it. Despite all that, I stand tall and proud of the Sikh identity. Notwithstanding, I have been celebrated and honoured for it.

"Mankind's religious future may be obscure; yet one thing can be foreseen. The living higher religions are going to influence each other more than ever before, in the days of increasing communication between all parts of the world and the branches of human race. In this coming religious debate, the Sikh religion and its scriptures, the Guru Granth, will have something special of value to say to the rest of the world."

- Arnold Toynbee, British Historian

Today, just over 500 years after the faith was founded, how do we do in the Litmus test? *Sikhism*, in my eyes, needs a major overhauling due to a lack of continuous improvements, lessons learned, and not understanding the documented guidelines. These are all automotive/industrial terms used in the quality of a service or product, yet they ring true when we talk about this wonderfully open-minded faith/philosophy.

The *Sikh* faith has changed over the past century, and some might say that this new look is unfortunate. Due to external challenges being faced by the faith and influences considered to be harmful to its philosophy, our forefathers decided to establish the *Singh Sabha* movement in 1873. Then further controls and limitations were placed on the faith and its faithful when the *Sikh* code of conduct (*Reyat Maryada*) was initiated in the 1920s, developed in the 1930s, and finalized in the 1950s. Some will argue that this code of conduct changed the dynamics and acceptance of the *Sikh* faith for many. Additionally, the partition of India and the forming of Pakistan in 1947 further segregated and hindered the broader message of the faith, which separated many of those that felt a part of the *Sikh* religion.

Have we moved away, on an irreversible scale, from that relationship between the individual and the supreme energy, or are we fixated on outer elements, hoping they fill that inner void? There's no hiding it. The 1430 pages (*angs*) of the *Guru Granth Sahib*, the nearly 6,000 hymns (*shabads*), continuously tell us what we should be doing, how we should be living, what our primary focus should be, and how it should not just be about the external, but the inner journey. Globally, the current state of our *Gurdwara's* and what they are providing to the congregation, or should I say the lack thereof, is of the most significant concern to me. *Gurmukhi* (the language in which the *Guru Granth Sahib* is written) is today very much like Shakespearean English; one sees the similarity between the two, but boy oh boy, it can be challenging to understand some of those words. We, as *Sikhs*, were provided with the 11th *Guru* in a textual format, which allowed us to read and learn from it. Today that is not happening. Forget the diaspora and their children, I know that the clear majority of those born in India of the *Sikh* faith cannot understand what is being said. This must change, or we will lose the current and next generations of this faith. *Sikhism* is a universal faith, and for that reason alone, it should be shared among all. The sad fact is that we have not been able to share it amongst ourselves, and fear losing it to the vast majority. Losing what you may ask? The opportunity to take the journey within and feel the connections between you and all of humanity.

We need to take the inner journey. It needs to be carried out by the individual and it needs to start now. Begin to realize who you are as a person, and be truthful and honest because it is critical to moving forward.

My personal 'spiritual' journey continues. The spiritual global positioning system (SGPS) within me helps me to strive for self-improvement. The 'student 4 life' approach allows me to learn and understand innate thoughts and philosophies, and the teacher traits within me want me to share those with you.

The FIVE Virtues

Sat | Truth
Santokh | Contentment
Daya | Compassion
Nimrata | Humility
Pyaar | Love

The following portions of this chapter take you on a deeper dive into a practical understanding of vices and virtues, rather than a theological description rooted in medieval morality. The root of these personality traits, mindsets, or attitudes are generated within an individual. I am a firm believer that if thoughts and feelings are manifested for a prolonged period of time, they become your energy. Be it kind, respectful, tolerant, selflessness, cruel, insolent, prejudice, or selfish energy; these all affect both the individual and his/her environment, the question is, how do we control the vices and promote the virtues?

The real U has a strong moral compass, but one has to be aware of the drivers that can navigate you away from the light!

Let's go in-depth on some of the virtues and vices, such as humility, greed, attachment, contentment, love, and compassion, as I have understood them.

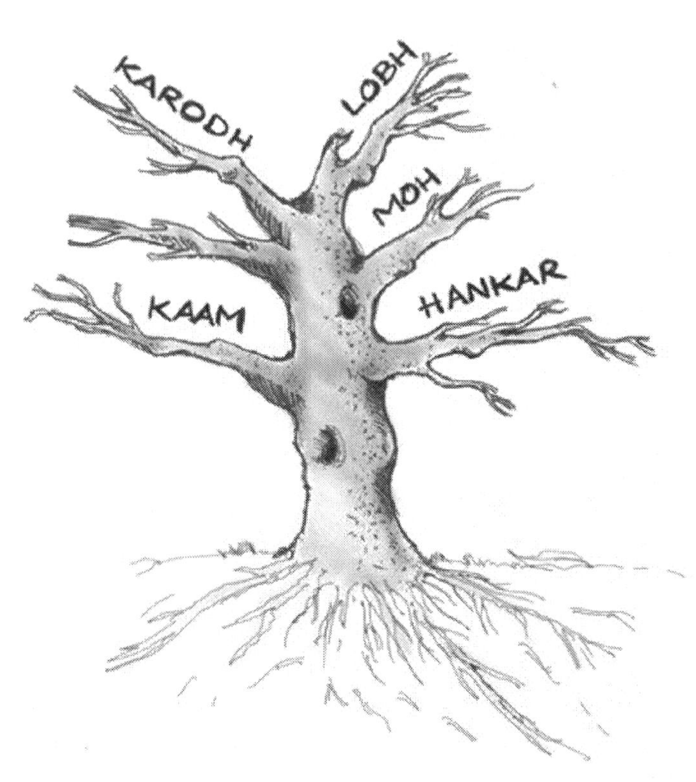

Kaam | Lust
Krodh | Anger
Lobh | Greed
Moh | Attachment
Hankaar | Ego

Illustration 14: A visual representation of the five vices vs. the five virtues by Kulbir Colin Singh Dhillon

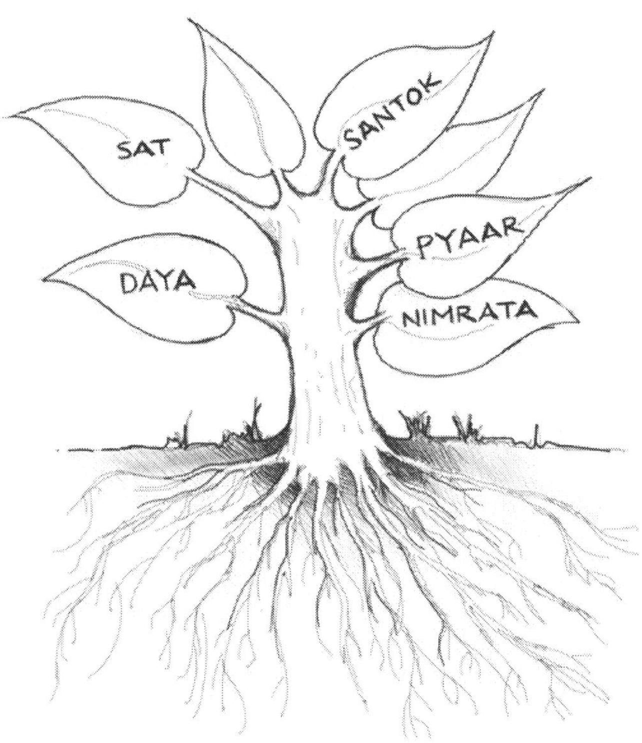

Sat | Truth
Santokh | Contentment
Daya | Compassion
Nimrata | Humility
Pyaar | Love

NIMRATA - *Humility* through Learning

To selflessly put the needs of others before your own is the essence of *Nimrata* (Humility). To be humble is to control one's ego and to save oneself from isolation on a perceived island of narcissism. It is an essential tool for experiencing life altruistically and appreciating that you are simply a small thread woven into the grand tapestry of life. To continue learning, and being open-minded to other's ideas, one has to be injected with an element of humility on the individual's part. I personally want to continue learning and to never feel that I have somehow reached a pinnacle of knowledge. For the past seven years, I am honoured to represent Canada as the only Canadian judge at the North American International Auto Show. Joining me are the Heads of Design studios from every global car maker. Our objective is to choose the year's best production and concept car designs. I am humbled to be in the presence of great studio design legends of our time like my friend, Ralph Gilles from Fiat Chrysler Automobiles. Though we are the same age, his understanding of design is beyond my years and therefore I will constantly ask him questions and advice around vehicle design and design philosophy, never as an equal, but rather as a student.

As previously mentioned, I have lectured on the subject of design for over a decade and have been in charge of design studios, marketing and communication, and research and development departments for a billion-dollar automotive company. Over the nineteen years of service at this global company, humility and perseverance were both critical ingredients of personal growth.

Today, I am a Chief Technical Office, helping to lead the digital transformation in the automotive sector for Canada, and guess what...I am still learning and listening to colleagues, and thanking them for advice, and more importantly, ensuring I give credit, where credit is due! I have always been well aware that I am no heliocentric heavenly body that others revolve around! Remember, humility should be sensed and felt by others based upon your actions.

Is there a litmus test for humility? Will questions from an emotional intelligence questionnaire assist in determining this? I truly don't know, but I will say that Ego (*Hankaar*) and Greed (*Lobh*) personality traits would need to be controlled and reduced in order for humility to gain a strong foothold.

Lobh, Santokh, & Pyaar - *Greed, Contentment & Love*

Greed (*Lobh*) is a selfish desire for excessive consumption of many things. To possess in excess of one's basic need with no consideration for others. Now, this net can be cast over a large portion of humanity, and some spend their entire lifetime in pursuit of becoming further entangled in it. Continents have changed hands in the quest of this driver as civilizations have been lost to it. This desire to own, consume, and have is not a new phenomenon. Greed has been a disease affecting humankind for eons. Some will argue the benefits of greed, being self-preservation and motivation, but let's be honest, the negative aspects hugely outweigh the positive ones.

In July 2016, I came across one of Joe Rogan Experience podcasts. He was interviewing the British comedian, actor and activist, Russell Brand. Now, Mr. Brand is a chap who wears his emotions and life experiences, like a tattoo, on his sleeves; an open book for all to peer in. At approximately the 50-minute mark in the interview, Joe asked Russell if he has been able to sustain that "high"; the sensation of something greater than himself - that feeling of bliss that he might have felt doing drugs, being a sex addict and so on. Russell's response made the hair on my arms and neck stand tall, he said that in fact, he feels those sensations and more when he is giving and sharing through altruism. Greed can be countered by tackling some of those driver traits one might have acquired. However, not everything is merely inherent. Habits and personality traits are formed and incubated in the environments we live in. When that selfish behaviour rears its ugly head, how often is it questioned by the elders in your environment? Is it reprimanded? Are we modelling it by following in the sinister footsteps of misguided mentors? Maybe they themselves practice greed? Greed *(Lobh)* is something that can affect us all. The question to ask is, how much does it affect us in the quest for self-realization?

The feeling of scarcity can make the world feel hostile and, in turn, make you feel like you are in competition with everyone else, possibly over resources that are probably more abundant than you realize. Being content could help control or limit the greed in our daily pursuits for personal growth.

If Contentment (*Santokh*) helps to neutralize greed, it can also provide the stillness needed to build up our means of preventing future relapses. Contentment can give us the breathing space required to develop a moral compass. In being content, we can look to sharing our own largesse with others who have less. Contentment is a stable bedrock for generosity to be built upon and sets the foundation for a more genuine and compassionate sense of charity.

"Contentment is natural wealth,
luxury is artificial poverty"
– Socrates

Love (*Pyaar*) is also required in helping to realign this misalignment. Love is the feeling that lets you know that we are all connected. In fact, we are all derived from the same source, like a billion drops of water, all calling the same large body-of-water, our point of origin. All living things are connected through love. We can agree that greed is injected with selfishness. It requires that we look through 'a *me* over *us*' lens. That separation promotes an ungenerous nature grounded in a false hierarchy. Once we begin to realize that there is no them but only us, that will also lessen the desire to continually want more. A technique to enable this mind-set change is to ruthlessly contemplate all actions, decisions and behavioural patterns on a daily basis. Pull yourself up and create a habit that develops into character. Only then will love succeed and it becomes prevalent.

I, personally, want to strive for success. I want to reach for a life that fulfils me spiritually and allows me to form healthy and nurturing relationships. There must be a balance in these states for my success in being adequately defined. I want to explore my parameters and expand my range of abilities. Can I make a documentary film? Let me try. Can I write a book? Hand me a pen. Nothing gets taken away from all that I am, but with every new skill, inherent abilities can only expand. The trick is to keep adding the positive while simultaneously removing the negative aspects/ingredients, those thoughts and feelings that hold you down and back. I have spent many a day looking inside myself to see if I have the hardware and components for what is termed a selfish individual. From my observation, I can tell you that I do. The solution, therefore, is to address this topic every-single-day of my life going forth. Quiet time/meditation, and the journey to go deeper within will also assist in both self-realization and the understanding that we are simply threads on a global tapestry. Another tool in one's kit for self-improvement is selfless service (*Seva*). Personally, the selfless service aspect of *Sikhism* was never something I shied away from, instead, I embraced it. I always felt an energy boost, a deep feeling of contentment from within while serving humanity. That feeling of contentment is precisely what I see as being prescribed as an antidote for greed. My journey for achieving success might stall upon pebbles of greed, on uneven and loose-footing surfaces of anger (*Krodh*), and the shards of ego (*Hankaar*). I slow down at these points and recalibrate my direction and intentions. I make sure that I stay true to my path and not be led astray by any driver's intent on changing my posture. I achieve my dreams on my terms, without disturbing the equilibrium of my ecosystem. My sights will always be on a spiritual plateau that leaves me feeling, and reaching, higher. I might hunger for success but on my spiritual, compassionate terms, and not those of a soulless society.

Daya – *Compassion*

Selfless service helps to unlock both Humility (*Nimrata*) and Compassion (*Daya*) in individuals. The act of serving without gain, but only for the betterment of the individual or humanity can only be powered by humility and compassion. There is no 'I' in this equation. We are all pre-wired with varying levels of both the positive and negative aspects of all these vices and virtues, and our personal journies are a constant exercise in amendments to the levels to best suit our personal desires and aspirations. Having little or no humility can cause our ego to overpower the person and the outcome is a conceited individual. Too little self-belief manifests as a lack of self-confidence, which can also hinder us from success. A scarcity of compassion can be apparent in cruel and greedy despots. Still, too much of it can empty and drain us so much that we have no energy left to sustain the other aspects of our lives (something that can be debated for many an hour!). Doing selfless service for all living beings should be a predisposition for us, but it gets frequently silenced. Ego, greed both help to suffocate the natural tendency in all of us to be more compassionate and humble.

The vices and virtues are part of our personality, separating the personality into specific traits is a part of the *Sikh* philosophy. Still, it is by no means exclusive to it. The delineations are common foundation stones of all the Indian subcontinent faiths, especially Buddhism. We are electromagnetic energy beings travelling within this vehicle and are made up of the five elements – earth, water, fire, air, and space. That energy field that keeps that one particular organ pumping blood throughout the body is electrified. It is our thoughts and feelings that make us up as an individual. Your chosen frequency of thought either allows you to feel positive or negative. The world in which we all live is, in fact, within our minds. It materializes outwardly daily and depending upon how much ruckus those thoughts and feelings are having in one's mind, your world could be a kaleidoscope of emotions. compassion can be a personal tool of directly easing any discomfort and pain one might feel; a shoulder to cry on and a helping hand.

We all should have the objective of being more compassionate. It very much is a contagious trait. like when you smile at someone or give way to others in the busy morning commute and then they too will do the same, thereby creating a domino effect.

The seeds of compassion planted in the human psyche need to be watered regularly to be activated. How does one make this happen? Selfless Service! To serve others. Selfless service or as we call it, *Niskam Seva*; when you expect nothing back. No favours, no gratitude, no recognition. Be secular and altruistic and practice selfless service at the hundreds of shelters for the homeless, seniors' centres, community centres, and charitable organizations that would welcome your time. Whether you volunteer at a pet rescue or a children's breakfast program, you should do this to add leaves to your tree. When you shelter a person in need and comfort them, those seeds of compassion blossom into a beautiful, welcoming, wise tree of compassion. My parents would take us on most weekends to a *Gurdwara* in Coventry, UK it was here that my education and training around serving others began.

When inside a *Gurdwara*, before entering the main hall (*Darbar*), everyone is asked to cover their heads and remove their shoes. The shoes can sometimes be scattered all over the place, and I recall my cousin and I organizing these shoes. It wasn't enough for us to simply place and arrange the shoes, no, we had to show our commitment to the philosophy by doing it in the most enthusiastic way that we could; we decided to purchase some shoe polish and buffing brushes and we began to clean the shoes too. When construction work was underway at the *Gurdwara* - and it was for several years - I became the extra set of hands passing house bricks to the bricklayer or unravelling and passing electrical wire to the electrician. No task was above or below me. Don't get me wrong, I was no angelic child, but that's precisely it …I do not think you need to be. There is no such thing, and you don't have to be a noble person to do good things. You just have to do selfless service when the opportunity presents itself, and you will eventually become a more compassionate, loving and humble individual. That invisible pedestal I referred to in the preface, keeps on getting toppled.

Selfless service became an integral part of my life. These days, it takes the form of helping to organize and run large charity events and organizations. In 2011, my friend, Tim Schmidt, started a charity car show to raise funds for cancer awareness. By 2015, Tim and Brenda's Place charity car show had raised over half a million dollars for Prostate Cancer Canada, and other charities, and became recognized as one of the largest one-day car shows in Canada!

What started as a seed in October 2009 as an exhibit at the Canadian House of Parliament, highlighting the role of the *Sikhs* as warriors and peacekeepers, germinated into the founding of The Sikh Heritage Museum of Canada. Today, the museum is bringing awareness to the greater Canadian community about the nation-building role of the *Sikhs* in Canada. I take great satisfaction in putting my efforts wholeheartedly into projects like this, an opportunity to help so many people; financially, emotionally and through awareness of the community. Selfless service requires that you find the time and commitment to put in all your effort and give it your very best. It needs to be built on a firm foundation of compassion, humility, and love. It's not always easy to find the time and energy between work and family commitments that are equally as important. Still, if you don't invest in caring for others, you are not truly investing in yourself. Are you reflecting on improving yourself? Are you committed to action? To achieve the goal of becoming selfless, you need to be more compassionate and loving to others. Why? It is for the common good of us all. Period!

"Bless me with Your Name, and make me content that the hunger of my mind be satisfied"

"Deh naam santokhia, utre man ki bhukh"

- Guru Granth Sahib, page 179

Moh – *Attachment*

According to most world religions, Attachment (*Moh*) has always represented the roots of one's self-inflicted limitation in life, particularly those from the Indian sub-continent. Being attached is to be rooted down, to be anchored, and restricted. Even the tree that represents the limit of oneself, the dead and decaying lifeless tree, has roots that make it challenging to extract, just like a decaying molar tooth that requires root canal surgery for extraction. Understand this limitation to be deep-rooted and sometimes steeped in tradition. It's the voice saying, "It's always been this way" and "It's in your DNA", when in fact this journey, we are all on, is our own and without limitations. It never has to be any particular way! Imagine deep seeds stuck firmly in soil; they will never grow and blossom into a rose or an oak tree if they don't shake themselves free of the damp cold soil and work their way up, breaking through the crust of soil. Similarly, attachment has the same effect in being that heavy wet soil on your spiritual journey to realizing your full potential. The roots provide the nourishment for all other aspects of thriving. Without attachment, greed does not receive a supply of energy. Your attachments can be to family, friends, objects, items, belonging, events, and situations, in varying degrees. There is an emotional feeling of loss when you detach yourself from an intense but unhealthy relationship—a sense of heartache that strikes you at your core. The self's reaction to detachment is more cerebral when it comes to disengaging from an object and may manifest as a feeling of intense loss or alienation. Next time keep a lookout for this. The reactions are a response to separation and are felt deeply, even when the attachment is the worst thing for you. Get to know yourself well enough to be able to calibrate your balance between being grounded and being dragged down.

Illustration 15: Sack of Rocks
by Kulbir Colin Singh Dhillon

Do not mistake your responsibility and love for your family and friends as being attachment. For many centuries, scientists have assumed that the animal world is a world of no emotion and they do not have the capacity to love and to develop structural relationships. The fact is, the animal world is full of examples where the parents provide total love and nurturing to their offspring, and then 'let go' and allow nature to take its course. That is an example of consciously or unconsciously understanding attachment.

Sikhism teaches us to live fully in this world. *Sikhs* are not to renounce it but instead, participate fully in the day-to-day aspects of it. We do this because attachment is driven by your conscious mind. In fact, all rooted physical attachments are inspired by that inner voice drawing upon the experiences and behavioural patterns that might have moulded you. Detachment does not have to preclude anyone from having meaningful relationships and a comfortable life. Instead, it implies that there is something greater out there. But to see it, we have to rest our gaze from what keeps us from looking up and out.

Let me share with you the story of my mother, who is no longer with us. At the age of 59, she was diagnosed with cancer and given only months to live. Five years later, she decided to go on her own terms and free from most attachments. Slowly but surely, like a sculptor chiselling away at a block of marble to gradually create a masterpiece, she disengaged from all the things that tethered her to this mortal coil. Attachment should be seen as a large piece of marble, using incorrect tools will have adverse effects on the piece you want to reveal. Hammering it too hard would potentially wreck or prematurely break the solid block, possibly preventing the sculptor from *working* it correctly. Oftentimes, this comes with hesitation and therefore, withdrawing full potential. Don't get me wrong. I'm not saying that my Mum was a perfect soul, a fully enlightened being, or an ideal artist of her life's composition. She was somebody who believed in herself and carried her convictions to their furthest extent. From my early childhood, I remember witnessing her inner spirit and her control of attachment. Her detachment in her final days and months of her life not only benefited her for the next chapter but also prepared her immediate family to emotionally and spiritually accept a life without her physical presence.

Truth (*Sat*), Contentment (*Santokh*), Compassion (*Daya*), Humility (*Nimrata*), Love (*Pyaar*), Lust (*Kaam*), Anger (*Krodh*), Greed (*Lobh*), Attachment (*Moh*), and Ego (*Hankaar*) are potential foundation stones of one's personality. They will either bring you closer to the real U or simply allow you to be lost in the deep dark jungle of society and one's mind. Recognizing these elements of self, will only then allow you to begin self-improvements, and eliminating traits that prevent one from growing and fulfilling one's full potential. Try this on a daily basis…it will benefit you and everyone around you.

Illustration 16: Ik Onkar
by Kulbir Colin Singh Dhillon

Randomness:

HOW DO YOU BREATHE?

Breathing is good for you, right...but are you REALLY breathing? "How do you breathe?" Might sound like an odd question, if not slightly crazy, but seriously, "How do you breathe or how about where do you breathe from?" Hmm, through my mouth and nose, you might say. Well, how about this; do you breathe from your chest area or deeper from the naval area? Oh, okay, now I get it.

Taking deeper breaths from the navel area helps to activate your *parasympathetic nervous system, letting the body recuperate and heal. Breathing deeply does equal less stress and a more positive outlook on life, not to mention giving those lungs a good work out, that does not always have to equate to a 25- mile bike ride. However, there's nothing wrong with doing that for physical and mental health. Still, diaphragmatic breathing increases your body's energy levels and a multitude of other benefits too. So, how do you breathe?

---

*The Parasympathetic Nervous System, also known as the digest and rest system, conserves energy by slowing the heart rate. It is also responsible for regulating the body's unconscious actions.

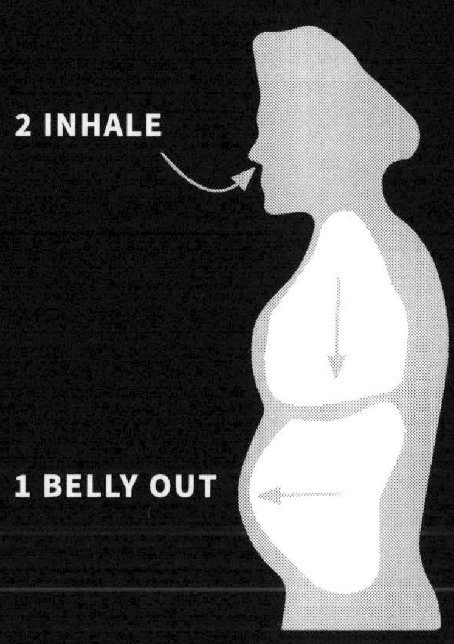

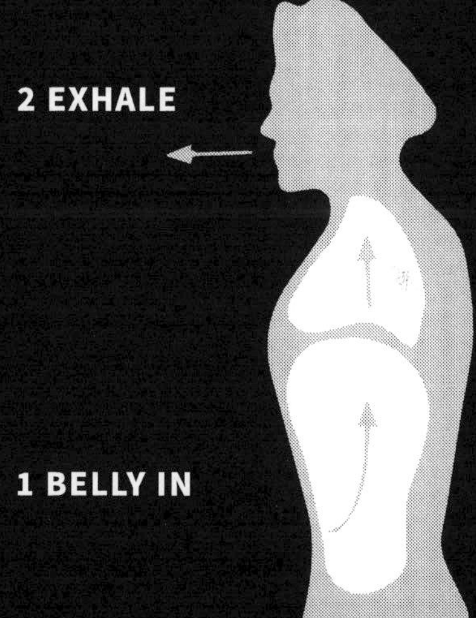

Illustration 17: How to clear your mind through breathing
by Kulbir Colin Singh Dhillon

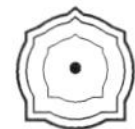

CHAPTER 11
"Yours, with the greatest possible sympathy...Charles"

Originally published in The Sikh Foundation International blog - July 2013

This book is a conglomerate of events that occurred through the current voyage of my life. Your high and low points in the journey are like pages of a book - they can last as long as it takes to flip a page or continue on until all chapters are completed. For some individuals, an ideal life should be utterly void of sorrow and pain. No such entity has ever existed, and nor should one assume it could. Emotionally trying times in one's life should not be seen as a catalyst for inner, mental hardship, instead, we need to build the resolve of one's self to navigate through these choppy waters, knowing that the journey does finally come ashore. The pages in that chapter have turned. Do not wait for the voyage to end before you begin to evaluate the situation. Instead, see opportunity in every circumstance, whether positive or negative, to grow and not be burdened by the baggage of victimized thoughts.

Photo: HRH Prince Charles with my late Mother (June 2013)
Courtesy of HRH Prince of Wales office.

The individual that brings you into this world, the life-giver who unconditionally loves you from her core, providing you security and selfless affection is your mother, which we often call Mum. Her tough love will make you a better person, and she will love and adore you till the end of time; a love unmatched by any other living being. This colossus human is the backbone of nature's model of nurturing and growth of all living things. When she leaves this earth, she will impact your life greatly and she should leave YOU intact and functional, not broken. The 21st of September 2020 marked the seventh year since my Mum passed away. I wanted to share a story from her final stage in life that gave her both comfort, satisfaction, and for her family, a story of when Mum met the future King of England!

"The casket should be closed. Do not bathe me. I have picked out my clothes (*Salwar Kameez*); don't buy me a new set, and do not bring my body home (traditional in the UK)". When she would talk about these details, we would all simply reply, "Yes, okay, Mum" not fully grasping the depth of support she was providing for her children and our Dad, just months before she finally left us. As the time grew nearer to my Mum's departure from this world, she began to prepare all of us for the next chapter. She wanted to support us through our most trying time. This was my Mum, *Gurbaksh Kaur Dhillon*, until the very end.

She was fearless and free from an early age; I have already shared her infamous story of killing the king cobra snake in the grain storage room. She was the youngest of seven, yet throughout her life, she was the voice of reason and authority to all of them. When she spoke... they all listened.

My Mum was a religious and spiritual being; she embraced her faith with open arms. She wanted her boys to be turban-wearing Sikhs (Sardars), and her wish was that we would stay connected to our faith and be proud of who we are, and of our rich cultural/spiritual heritage. She always challenged rituals and traditions surrounding some aspects of our culture and religion; little did we know that the biggest ritual she would challenge would turn out to be the one surrounding her passing.

Death is part of the journey we will all face. The general attitude to death, might I say, continues to be problematic/ underestimated for a lot of people. Death must be conquered by the individual and not feared. Yes, I know it is easier said than done, so what would be required to create such a mindset? A strong faith in self? To be spiritually awoken maybe? What I do know is that for over five years, ever since my Mum was diagnosed with cancer in 2008, she never once felt 'victimized'. The question, "why me?" was never asked. She would say, "Your dad has been good to me, you boys have turned out well, I'm just going home now…" She understood that life is simply a journey - an experience to be had - but not owned. In order to live this way, you must have unwavering faith in yourself and your own beliefs, something she possessed in abundance.

After hearing about this final chapter of my Mum's life, I wrote an article about her meeting with His Royal Highness, The Prince of Wales, called, "The visit from the future King of England" for the late Dr. *Narinder Singh Kapany's* organization, The *Sikh* Foundation, as a piece which helps us all to challenge the nonsensical rituals and traditions we are surrounded by. The takeaway lesson from this chapter should be to question all rituals and traditions that we so blindly follow. Because my Mum questioned, she allowed us all to begin celebrating her life immediately. Because she challenged the norms of our culture, she provided us all with the strength to accept her passing and carry on living this life we have been given.

On the 17th of June 2013, Mum was stabilized again to the point that the Marie Curie Hospice in Solihull, UK decided to send her home from Palliative care. When my Dad went to complete her paperwork for discharge, and make a small donation due to how well the staff had taken care of her, the young lady provided some fascinating information. "It's a shame Mrs. *Dhillon* will be leaving before HRH, the Prince of Wales' visit, to officially open the Hospice, Mr. *Dhillon*", she said. When returning to my Mum's room and sharing the news with both her and Cindy, my Mum flat out said, "I'm not going home till I see Charlie".

Dad suggested that my Mum should speak to the nurses and staff personally to see if they would extend her stay, but he didn't think it was possible since the discharge paperwork was already completed for the 19th of June, just two days before the HRH arrived. When the nurse came into the room, Mum said, "Charlie is coming. I'm not going". "Yes, Mrs. *Dhillon*, Prince Charles is coming this Friday, but I'm afraid your paperwork is already complete for you to go home on Wednesday, but let's talk with the Hospice Manager", as she moved around the room, checking supplies and materials, "let me see what they can do love".

Later that morning, the Hospice Manager came by the room. "Morning Mrs. *Dhillon*. How you are doing today?" "Good, thank you.", Mum replied "I heard you want to see the Prince of Wales?"

"Yes", said Mum.

"Well, why don't we do this. Why don't we change the date you will be discharged to Friday late afternoon after His Royal Highness leaves, and also the Prince's team have asked us to identify two patients for him to meet…why don't we add you to that list, hey?"

"Thank you", Mum said with her eyes filling with tears and her hands brought together in the *Sikh* way of greeting and being appreciated. Those tears in the eyes of a lioness were not of being star-struck, but rather of a citizen of the United Kingdom who has worked extremely hard to build a life of plentiful and by doing so, they helped to support this country. Those tears were droplets of redemption for all of those years of being racially abused, of being made to feel unwelcome and unwanted in this land.

My Mum was very rarely quiet. She would light up the room with her so-called knowledge of "anything and everything", for which she will forever be remembered for. She was a *real* person. In the final chapter of her life, she set a standard for all to witness and appreciate. She left the world as she had lived it; fearlessly, positively, and without objection.

"To reach your True Home after you die, you must conquer death while you are still alive."

"muiaa jit ghar jaieeaai tiit jeevadhiaa mar maar".

~ Guru Granth Sahib, page 21

As the quote (*Tukh*) from the *Guru Granth Sahib* above says, 'You must conquer death whilst you are still alive'. I believe Mum achieved this.

On Friday 21st of June 2013, it only took less than nine-minutes for, His Royal Highness Prince Charles, a man who must meet thousands of people, to be touched by my Mum. For the next three, months Mum would regularly receive a call from the Prince's office checking in on her, on behalf of HRH, and wishing her a speedy recovery.

In the early hours of Saturday 21st of September, Mum peacefully left her earthly abode, her vehicle of expression. She left the same way she had lived - content and with much dignity. Though the 64 years she lived here on earth seem to be short to us, her loved ones, if you sit back and observe her journey, she did, in fact, live a beautiful and fulfilling life, and she lived it in absolute control. I received the call from my brother late on the evening of the 21st. On the morning of Saturday 22nd, I had a previously scheduled meeting with a local Member of Parliament on behalf of the Sikh Heritage Museum of Canada, regarding a proposal to Canada Post. 2014 was going to be the 100th anniversary of the *Komagata Maru* incident when Canada refused the immigration of 376 passengers from India. This was an important milestone for both Canadians and *Sikhs* globally. I got up that morning and led the meeting, and then returned home, probably not the right thing to do as far as *society* was concerned. Why did I go? Because that is exactly what my Mom would have expected; to put service to society ahead, of oneself.

On Friday 4th of October 2013, a delivery was made to our family residence in Birmingham, England. A bouquet of white roses and lilies in a brown rectangle cardboard box and a self-sealed manila document envelope was hand-delivered. The day after the bouquet and envelope arrived, a senior nurse from the hospice paid us a visit. She shared with us how Prince Charles had asked to be kept "up-to-date" with Mrs. *Dhillon's* condition. She further said that the flowers and letter should not be taken as a simple gesture, as it was not common practice. The particular delivery that had arrived was from HRH Prince Charles.

I have a theory that a person's electromagnetic energy can be stronger than his/her spoken word or any facial/body expression that may be created. Sometimes we think the 'connection' we make with another individual is based on the spoken words shared between both parties. Maybe that's true in some cases, but how about the connection of your energy; the real U?

Scientists are now describing how the heart, which is a muscle, is surrounded by an electromagnetic field that pulsates and keeps us all ticking. That same electromagnetic field encompasses our bodies too. It was not my mum's broken English' or the fact she accidentally called him Charlie that connected her with HRH that day in June, but their energy…everyone in the room bared witness to! To His Royal Highness, Prince Charles, on behalf of Mr. *Rashpal Singh Dhillon* & family; thank you for honouring the life of my Mum, *Gurbaskh Kaur Dhillon.*

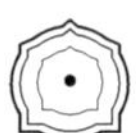

Photo: Copy of the condolence letter to my father from HRH Prince of Wales.

BIRKHALL

1st October, 2013

Dear Mr. Dhillon,

Having had the great pleasure of meeting your dear wife when I visited the Marie Curie Hospice in Solihull a few months ago, I just wanted to say how terribly sorry I was to hear the very sad news that she had recently passed away. I can only begin to imagine what an enormous gap she will leave in the life of yourself and your family and particularly wanted you to know how deeply I feel for you.

It was a great joy to have met you all back in June, despite such difficult circumstances for your poor wife. I am so relieved, however, to learn that she died at home, as I recall she was so looking forward to being at home – surrounded by those she loved.

You and your family are so much in my thoughts and prayers at a time of such loss and anguish.

Yours, with the greatest possible sympathy —

Charles

THE THREE HOUSES·THE THREE HOUSES

CHAPTER 12
Creativity in All

Creativity is the transformation of an idea into reality. It also entails being able to transcend thoughts that can be described as standard and normal. The definition of creativity is broad and should stay that way. To pigeon-hole creativity into silos would be unjust and dampening.

So who are the creative people? Well, we are all creative beings. We all innovate and create throughout our lives. Whether we use existing materials and reform them to give shape to an idea, or we write or compose something seemingly out of thin air, we all have the potential to engage in the act of creativity. Some of us are compelled to do it daily, while others less frequently, nevertheless, we all have the capacity to become creative, with greats ideas, and be artistically inclined.

What is the source of one's creativity? Where does it come from and how does one manifest it? How about from within; the source of all potential...energy (the real "U")! Whether you are Albert Einstein, Elon Musk, Isaac Newton, Naveen K. Jain, Nikola Tesla, Steve Jobs, Walt Disney, Leonardo Di Vinci,

Dr. *Narinder Singh Kapany*, Jay-Z, or any number of recognized creative geniuses, past or present, the source of this 'need to make something out of nothing' comes from within. And within is where the real "U" resides, which is connected to that cosmic power source, making it a spiritual experience at its essence.

"If you want to find the secrets of the universe, think in terms of energy, frequency and vibration"

– Nikola Tesla

How does my creative decision-making differ from others? I am not really sure that it does. If we think of the lotus flower that starts its life buried in murky waters. It struggles through the detritus to rise above and bloom unsullied. The lotus flower is often used as a metaphor to describe the separation of the spiritual from the temporal world. We have to fight our way through the weaknesses, sufferings, and temptations that can tangle us and keep us down. Notwithstanding, we must always aim to rise above. We have to remember our roots, but still ensure that we maintain a higher state of consciousness that shows our evolution of thought. It is that separation that needs to occur for the creative process to be engaged and ignited in oneself. A separation that allows you to engage with the inner you...the real U. How does one realize and recognize the real U? One must be prepared to spend some quiet time (meditative state) and connect with the creative creator within. It is akin to asking a question to yourself and having the courage and patience to wait for the answers to start streaming in. My creative process is germinated within and extends outwards for growth and inspiration.

Planting Seeds of Creativity

I vividly remember a short project I once had at university. I was asked to review a car, any type of car, and suggest a design improvement. This was only a two-day project. The exhaust system (muffler and tip) was always an eyesore zone for me. The vehicle I chose was the Honda Civic; its body styling was quite acceptable for the era (early 1990s), but on the rear of the vehicle was the muffler, which was turned 90 degrees, so you could bear witness to the whole damn vessel. This was also the era when the car body did not sit as low as some cars do today, thereby making the contraption stand out like a sore thumb. My suggestion was to bring the body styling lower on the rear of the vehicle, and if possible, incorporate the muffler/exhaust pipe into the rear bumper/fascia. That is now a standard practice in the automotive industry for almost close two decades!

Problem-solving, designing "stuff" and generally dreaming up ideas in my mind's eye began quite early on for me. Looking back, I was probably seven or eight years old when I started connecting with my creativity. I assumed that everybody thought in the same way I did. Maybe they did, but the usual feeling that our creative senses are limited, is typically focused around the final execution of the act; whether it is dancing, composing, cooking, building, or painting and drawing. If you don't have the foot skills, the hand/finger movements that others have, or the initial ideas, we tend to stop and label it as unsuccessful ...I can't do it.

"Keeping the child inside alive, keeps the artist close by"
- Kulbir Colin Singh Dhillon

Creativity for me means that I had the ability to see solutions in my mind. I can assemble and disassemble objects and visualize them in three-dimensions (3D). The next step was to extract the ideas and thoughts and lay them on paper. I seemed to have a natural ability for drawing and sketching. Problem-solving needs to be understood by those around you too; this can be done in its most basic form, through the medium of language, hand gestures, or sketching out your ideas. These techniques are important in conveying the exact information to bring designs to fruition. Expressing one's inner vision through the medium of drawing or verbal imaginative descriptions is part of the creative process. Whether you are sitting behind a desk or working on a construction site or keeping society safe through janitorial services, creativity must be accessed and applied regularly. Just because the label isn't visible, doesn't mean it is not happening!

The creative process for solving a problem not only becomes the answering of that original design brief, but also developing a solution or product that does not infringe upon anyone else's intellectual property.

As illogical and irregular as some creative geniuses seem to be, I had found that the creative process is very systematic;

from the initial problem being identified to the steps to solving the problem or situation. Though my training may have been in Industrial Design, my years of experience have helped to highlight one simple thing; that many job descriptions have a process that creatively allows you to visualize and understand. For example, I am writing a book. I have no professional or academic training in writing or storytelling, yet here I am, about to be a published author. This book and other "non-industrial design" projects are further proof of creativity in action. In most places, creativity can be seen or assumed. Take, for example, the home, how do you take your *builder's beige* walls and standard décor house and make it your *home*? Unknowingly, we all use decisions governed through creativity. The simple choice of wall-colouring or covering is a page out of the creative bible. It is a natural phenomenon, which all humans can partake in. As people, we have pigeon-holed it and described those that have furthered their education in the field of creativity, or those that have made a mark on society through other channels, as the only creative folk. It is tangible and does not require genetic inheritance, rather it simply requires a passion and understanding of the medium one chooses, and a possible connection to the real U... the inner U.

How do I implement creativity on a daily basis?

I feel creativeness allows one to take calculated risks and the willingness to attempt certain feats. I was in charge of global marketing and a company's design studio for several years, and the only connection or experience I had in marketing, prior to being given the responsibility, was an undergraduate degree thesis paper, which I prepared on the relationship between industrial design and marketing. But because I'm not risk-evasive and was calculated in my innovation process, I never felt like I did not connect with the subject matter. Instead, it was seamless and connected. Decisions for all the departments were made with a broad imaginative palette, and a decent size toolkit of ideas, to support the decisions. These were all attributes of embracing the creativity within.

Another example might be my work with the Sikh Heritage Museum of Canada. I have always been a student of history since my first visit to the library. In fact, history was one of the building blocks of my young creative life. Seeing all those examples of early man creating tools for himself, and those magnificent architectural buildings and structures, that defy the simplistic tools with which they might have been built, motivated me. The foundation stone of my relationship with the Sikh Heritage Museum of Canada started in 2008, when Mr. *Kalra*, and I decided to put together a *Sikh* heritage exhibition in the Canadian Parliament West block building called The Spirit Born People exhibition. (The Royal Ontario Museum commissioned the globally renowned Singh Twins to create a painting titled, 'Sikhs in Canada' which pays homage to the exhibit). We pored over images, choosing the right ones to tell the visual story of the Sikhs serving in global wars. We created new written content to accompany the visual narratives. It was our responsibility to make sure that the look and feel of the exhibition, along with the booklet to support it, was of a high standard and engaging to all visitors. The finished product and the accolades were humbling. The driving force that guided this project was creativity in full display. It was the adhesive that held together all the components and pulled them together into a cohesive whole. Over the years, that same attitude and approach has allowed me to create several successful events at some of the largest car manufacturers in the world. After one particularly successful event, I was told that our exhibit is now the new benchmark for all others to attain. The driving force again is creativity, unstifled, and free to shape change and to create your own path!

One thing is for sure, my mind was in perpetual motion. Yes, I know the average person has approximately 50,000 thoughts a day, however, we need to pay attention to the number of thoughts entering and exiting our minds, in order to focus. It requires clarity to accomplish what you need to be successful. Can clarity thrive amidst clutter? The mind of a person functions much like a hard drive or cloud storage. It has the capacity to store multiple files and projects. The brain can sort the information according to the degree of importance, yet it still controls the other chattering of the mind.

If I go to the movies to watch a new film, I tend to go alone. I am a lover of all things creative. I see the creative process in everything we engage in. It is as much a part of preparing a meal as it is of earning a living by being a creative designer. Films are beautiful and are artistic compositions. Sounds, images, and colours, strum on our emotional strings using human nature as a plectrum. I go on my own because I want to be completely engrossed in the experience without the distraction of a companion undergoing their own connection with the art form. I am very observant, I notice small details in the background, the costumes, and the environment being presented. They may or may not be what the artist has worked so hard at in drawing the attention of one's eyes, but I will look to figure out these things and this is all done naturally, without force. I apply what I see to my own caché of materials to draw upon when I am inspired, consciously, and storing in the sub-conscious. It comes as second nature to me. This is what happens when you are in sync with your own creative nucleus; the real U.

How to become more Creative

It is not something that I consciously try and do, it is like anything else in life. I strongly feel that one can become more creative if they truly want to. Using the tech world as an analogy, to update the printed circuit board (PCB) or central processing unit (CPU), you need to add a compatible chip or card. Human beings are not too different. Listen to podcasts, read or listen to books, throw in travel (post-COVID-19 maybe) for some life experience and your *system* can be updated/refreshed.

If you are not failing, then you are not creating!

When researching about creativity and being or becoming more creative, the following are normally discussed: Your environment, imagination, music, reading, sketching, and aspirations for taking risks. I choose to finish the sentence with taking risks and exiting our comfort zone. This mindset is essential for creativity. To be innovative is to create unsuccessful and successful creations. Failure is an essential component of this process. Risk-taking, takes courage, confidence, and calculated implementation, but like skydiving or public speaking, it becomes slightly easier and the risks become less the more you engage in those activities.

MAKE THE
PHYSIOLOGICAL
CHANGE

TESTOSTERONE
VS
CORTISOL

Illustration 18: Testosterone vs. Cortisol
by Kulbir Colin Singh Dhillon

Physiologically, risk-taking, enthusiasm, and confidence are all signs of your body's chemicals, such as testosterone increasing and your cortisol levels decreasing. Testosterone is a hormone associated with power and cortisol is known as the stress hormone. If you approach the risk-taking portion of the creative process without fear and instead embrace the challenge, and you do so feeling somewhat confident and comfortable in doing it, even if you fail, it will become a lesson, sometimes a very valuable one and a path to success.

How to realize Creativity

Like air, creativity surrounds us. It is not just about being artistic, it's more about having a certain attitude. Are you ready to embrace failure? Are you willing to take risks? These are critical personality traits that one must possess. What kind of work do you do? What is your career path? Whether you are working in a fast-food restaurant or the CEO of a technology start-up company, using creativity in your approach to assigned tasks, can only enhance both the activity and the outcome.

Be sure to be equipped with all the right defiance mannerisms needed for living a more creative life. Do not fear the unknown, of not understanding the beginning, or not being able to see the end. Let the dopamine flow and the testosterone levels rise. Read more, read those things that interest you, those subject matters that can enhance you, and those fields that can help to complete you. Keep a journal, write down thoughts, daily events, and desires. Sketch down your thoughts and ideas too.

Remember, it is not about a god-given talent or your DNA, but about seeing things clearly. A great example of this is Matthew McConaughey's book, *Greenlights*. It's the extracted nectar of 35 years of him journaling, and understanding all the times life gave him red lights, yellow lights, and green lights!

For over a decade, I have taught designers and technical/ engineering students how to capture their ideas on paper. I kept it very rudimentary, using paper, pencils, and pens to enhance those lines which describe an emotion. The classrooms of designers were more competent at drawing, versus the room full of technicians and engineers. It was the challenge of teaching the latter group that I realized the importance of truly seeing, both the physical object in front of oneself, and seeing the innovative idea in one's mind's eye - are both hugely critical for the creative process.

To think that when we look at an object, for example, a 550ml bottle of water (without a cap in this case), and we all see the same thing, could not be further from reality. Not everyone sees the number of threads for the cap, not everyone sees the parting line from the blow moulding process, and not everyone considers the thickness of the material on the top edge (neck of the bottle). Still, when these features are pointed out, it turns on an internal switch within the individual. Not because they might not have seen this, or had it merely pointed out, but because of what has now happened to the sketch they were creating. These additional details and numerous others can make the drawing and its creators look and feel more complete and vibrant. Yes, the vertical lines might not be very straight or the ellipses too "fish-like", those things can be improved, but the fact that they must look closer, and ask questions about what is in front of them, allows them to take that visualization practice to another level. So, when they think of a design within their mind's eye, they begin to do the same exercise; break it down into details, and make their idea visually and creatively stronger.

By using the practice of visualization I witnessed the growth in not only their sketching ability but also within their creativity, in assigned projects, hitting a trajectory, which was something I had never witnessed before. I personally have experienced growth in my own creativity, I have been an instrument in the development of others' creativity, and all the while I do this through the support of the REAL me...that energy which resides within all, so No. More. Excuses. Please!

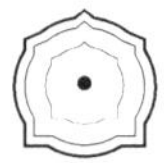

CHAPTER 13
STUDENT 4 LIFE

"Education is the kindling of a flame,
not the filling of a vessel"
- Socrates

My grandfather was a headmaster in rural *Punjab*, India. He had told his sons that his pension was to be used to help others and that they were to support the upkeep of the family properties. I also remember the stories of his bicycle journeys to and from the villages he taught in, sometimes travelling over five miles each way, every day (I am sure uphill too). My recollection of my retired headmaster grandfather was one of an elderly *Sikh* man, dressed in a tailored *kurta pajama* (traditional clothing for men in the Indian subcontinent), supported with a waistcoat. His pocket watch and chain accessorize his outfit, along with his reading glasses that were placed in his top right breast pocket. He would always have a pile of books sitting on a side table, next to the large Victorian-style armchair he sat in. Another tower of books was kept beside his bed. His favourite books were about what I now know as spirituality; the education of the soul.

As previously mentioned, my father was a technical drafting and fine art teacher in the 1960s. In my second visit to India, in 1983, I was able to see first-hand, my father's sketches, paintings, and technical illustrations, which I brought back with me to the UK for safekeeping.

Despite his own father's love of the written word, I did not see my dad reading a lot when I was growing up. Not newspapers and certainly not books. As I got older, I began to understand why. The daily bickering of politics did not interest him. Do not get me wrong, you could set a wristwatch to the accuracy of our family converging around the TV to watch the 6:00 PM news, yet, reading about his homeland, the *Punjab* and, its politics did not interest him in the least. Neither did biographies nor non-fictional works. The only books that engaged my Father and my Mother were those based on *Sikhism*, the spiritual scriptures themselves, and supporting material, like Stories related to the times of the *Sikh Gurus (Sakhis).*

My own first set of books were borrowed from Great Bridge Public library in 1977. I vividly remember a massive volume titled, The History of the World as being one of my first books. My Dad obviously picked it out for me. Some of the words and their meanings were beyond my understanding, yet the photographs and images of the history of mankind were compelling to me. The vivid, ghostly image of the Sutton Hoo helmet, an example of Anglo-Saxon amour from the 7th century A.D, has stayed with me.

"Mr. Dhillon, if Colin puts his mind to it, he can achieve anything", was a sentence that was shared with my father several times by my teachers, throughout my childhood. The fact is that if anyone puts his or her mind to it, the impossible becomes possible. Let us just say that I never reached my academic potential, especially at high school. Though, that volume of *The History of the World* started a pattern for me, of picking up books that I delved into for the pictorial introduction to historical events, rather than the words. I did not enjoy English until it was taught to me by a young teacher, who somehow made it less formal and more engaging. I did find the learning occurred when the teacher was passionate about the subject and not forcefully shoved down my throat. I am still to this day in touch with a few of my teachers, one from public junior school and two others from high school. They have all impacted my life in a big way. They all taught with a deep-rooted passion and engaged the learning molecules within me.

The passion for teaching is in my DNA you could say. The process of ingraining a subject that I truly care about into the hearts and minds of students takes days, if not weeks or months. Learning occurs from focusing your senses, and feeling the learning, via the exchange of curiosity and electromagnetic energy. It may seem a bit radical and slightly 'out there', but my record of success states that it works. Whether I am teaching Design Management, Ergonomics/Human Factors, Design Theory or Rendering, my goal is to extract the best work from my students and for them to understand and absorb the content.

I make it clear to them that I am here to support their learning, and that I am available after the class/course is over. I have a firm but fair approach to my academic teaching style; I try and focus on all my students, knowing that everyone, once they have overcome the mental block that "I cannot do this" surface layer, can develop and produce work initially not perceived by them. It is called energy centred learning and it is a spiritual process.

"Learn from yesterday, live for day, hope for tomorrow. The important thing is not to stop questioning."
- Albert Einstein

As introduced towards the end of the previous chapter, a few years ago, whilst teaching design thinking to some technical engineering students, I had one of those *eureka* moments. I was challenged with teaching non-design students to present ideas on paper like designers. This was always challenging. Typically, I have a class of thirty students, all with different levels of drawing/sketching abilities. Each year, I would have at least half a dozen students that felt really challenged with most of the in-class and regular assignments, because they all felt they could not draw. Now, I did state earlier that my brother and I both would have been expected to be good at drawing. Why? Because our father was. The same set of DNA ran through our system, as did his. But that is not entirely true. I have two children of my own, and although my daughter seems quite artistically inclined, my son struggles to draw or sketch.

I decided to change the way I teach this subject matter and ask each student to do the following; to visualize what they were about to draw. Most of the earlier classes required the students to draw already manufactured products. This persistent request for them to see what was in front of them was quite astonishing. At the end of the fourteen-week semester, the growth and ability of each student was humbling. All because I asked them to see, to look closer, and closer. This visualization process in-class was quite spiritual at times… a constructive energy encapsulated the group. I bring a certain energy, like anyone else, when conducting a class of learning. Based on my attitude and my energy (positive/negative or high/low) level, one can begin to predict the outcome.

My approach to teaching was always to limit the amount of time I continually lectured. The magic number I felt, was twenty minutes of continuous talking while the students listened. After that period, I would either open up the room for a Q&A session or begin the in-class assignment. This process of learning under guidance and support, and the eureka moments felt by individual students, who might have been able to achieve a level of learning or understanding (mentally or physically), had an air of spirituality; a connection to something greater than the sum of individuals within that classroom.

The word *Sikh* translated into English means, *student*. I truly feel that I am a student for life. I am always willing to learn. Willing is the keyword. I want to grow. I have a thirst for all knowledge.

My head is full of so many useless things, yet I want to continue the quest to fill it with so much more. I have lectured for over 12 years and have helped establish classes and organizations in the name of higher learning. My biggest and most important development project is learning about who I am, achieved innately through a yearning for insight, self-development, and improvement, which is driven by my thirst for knowledge. In order for me to understand the universe and all that resides within it, I need to understand myself.

Society needs to actively promote the concept of *student for life.* When I was growing up, you were only a student until you quit school at 16, or left college, or university. That is when your so-called education ended. You were sent off on your own with the advice to muddle through the rest alone. Most would figure something out about life, but really it is like being pushed into a forest with no map, compass, or smartphone, to help navigate your way out.

I have just celebrated a major milestone in my life, where my date of birth is suggesting that I am twenty years older than I feel... yes, I just turned 50! I hope that I can continue to be a student all my life. That my life of learning continues and that I do not put up any barriers to new ideas. Though I may be a CTO, I'm always open and happy to learn new ideas and to be taught if and when needed. I want the excitement and passion for new ideas to be my constant companion. My education, career choices, and the selfless service (*Seva*) in my community are all like books within my internal bookcase. My search for true knowledge and the answers to life can be found in the "reference publications" and "endless footnotes" that help to understand the real me.

Illustration by Nipun D Kasote

THE THREE HOUSES·THE THREE HOUSES

THE DÉCOR

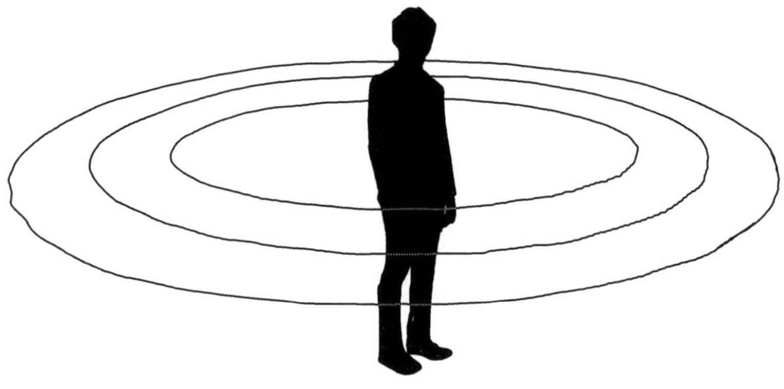

Illustration 19: Your aura radiates over twenty feet in diameter
by Kulbir Colin Singh Dhillon

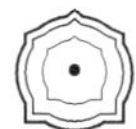

CHAPTER 14
We Are Energy Beings

After the events of 2004 through to 2007 (see Chapter 10, *Fake Fakir*: Thank You), not only was I emotionally and physically exhausted, I was completely disillusioned with religion. I had fought a battle that spanned continents to get justice for the *fake fakir's* victims, and for the most part, without the support of our religious leaders. I wanted to be numb from my past urges for self-improvement. No longer had I any interest to continue finding the answers to life, rather I just wanted to live a bland normal life - just exist and not worry about this existence, or invest in what might come after. This period lasted between twelve to fourteen months and was fueled by my anger and resentment towards religious leaders and religion, and with all of its nonsensical trappings. Anyone that was willing to listen (few poor souls that had no choice but to listen) was bombarded with my negativity and anger of all religious things. I could never completely eliminate that inner voice connection to something deeper within.

That magnetic pull towards spirituality, that yearning to fill the void within. Have you ever wanted something so badly that it hurts? Something materialistic or a person's love? You want it and you desire it more than anything at that present moment. Yet, once you obtain that thing, you realize that there still seems to be an inner void, a space within that needs to be filled. Even after the religion within me was dying, an eternal energy force within kept on pulsating. As much as I tried, I couldn't ignore it. It craved reconciliation with my soul. My personal experiences might have changed my mindset, and opened my eyes towards some aspects of organized faith, in manipulative ways, but the energy force within me was steadfast. I did what I hadn't done before; I decided to read about spirituality and the message of the Masters myself, so I could go deeper into my own self and try to understand my faith. This time I was taking the journey with only a single guide; the energy force that resides within all of us, which is not separate from any of us. Yes, a common blueprint within all entities.

I focused on the Root Verse (*Mul Mantaar*): The opening lines to the *Sikhs* 11th *Guru, Guru Granth Sahib.* They epitomize the teachings of the founder of the *Sikh* philosophy, *Guru Nanak Dev Ji.*

Mul Mantaar (Root Verse);

Ik - There is ONE(Ik) reality, the origin and the source of everything. The creation did not come out of nothing. When there was nothing, there was ONE, Ik.

Onkaar - When Ik becomes the creative principal it becomes Onkaar. Onkaar manifests as visible and invisible phenomenon. The creative principle is not separated from the created, it is present throughout the creation in an unbroken form, 'kaar'.

Satnaam - The sustaining principle of Ik is Satnaam, the True Name.

Kartaa Purakh - Ik Onkaar is Creator and Doer (Kartaa) of everything, all the seen and unseen phenomenon. It is not just a law or a system, it is a Purakh, a Person.

Nirbhau - That Ik Onkaar is devoid of any fear because there is nothing but itself.

Nirvair - That Ik Onkaar is devoid of any enmity because there is nothing but itself.

Akaal Moorat - That Ik Onkaar is beyond Time (Akaal), and yet it is existing. It's a Form (Moorat) which does not exist in Time.

Ajooni - That Ik Onkaar does not condense and come into any birth. All the phenomenon of birth and death of forms are within it.

Saibhang - That Ik Onkaar exists on its own, by its own. It is not caused by anything before it or beyond it.

Gurprasaad - That Ik Onkaar expresses itself through a channel known as Guru and it is only its own Grace and Mercy (Prasaad) that this happens.

(Mul Mantaar translated by, Harminder (Harry) Singh Mann)

Read it over again. What is he describing when he talks about the origin and source of everything? The visible and invisible, the seen and unseen, and the fact that there is nothing but itself. A form that does not exist in time. My interpretation of *Mul Mantaar* is *Guru Nanak* describing energy; uncontained and always present within and around all living entities.

In his TEDx talk in Cambridge, England (2011), Jeff Lieberman shared the following, which I paraphrase. *'We are a community of* 50 *trillion cells doing a magic dance. When seen through a microscope, it declares* 20 *trillion atoms. So, you're a community of* 1,000 *trillion, trillion atoms. Look even closer, and they all begin to fade away, and all that is left is vibrating energy!'*...Pure energy.

You are electromagnetic energy (EME); even that clay house you reside within, that to isn't solid substance, nothing is. Yet, the vast majority of us are naïve about this truth. How do we discover – tap into this energy bank...the real U?

The first law is to know oneself. We prefer living in a state of denial rather than getting to know ourselves. We choose to fast-forward through daily life and surround ourselves with distractions from the moment we are awake. Once in the car or on public transit, the headphones are in, or your nose-deep into a book. At work, colleagues or associates, and work in general, create the distraction. Don't get me wrong, some of this is valuable, but stay with me on this. Now in reverse on the journey home. Phew, no time for me... It's always go, go, go!

Why is that? Why all the distractions rather than more silence in our lives? Within internal silence lies so many gifts - de-stressing, creativity, finding answers to many life challenges. In this deep, dark, vast ocean of hush dwells, the real U!

Supporting Story.

I have never had much luck with my analog watches, you know, the non-digital kind. For as long as I can remember, my watches would last for about four to six months before the watch stopped working. I put this down to the fact that I didn't really splash the cash to buy decent watches. Once, my brother *Rajesh* gave me his Rotary analog watch to wear as part of an accessory for a trainee high school teacher when I was completing my postgraduate in Education back in 1997. The watch was a 5th year wedding anniversary present to him from my sister-in-law, *Rani*. I guess he had acquired an even better watch to wear than the Rotary. My brother has always had a fondness for good quality apparel and accessories, so I took it gladly. I had only worn it for a few weeks when it suddenly stopped ticking, so I immediately took it to the local watchmaker on Castle Street in Dudley, West Midlands. I was told to come back after a few days and pick it up, which I did. I was expecting to pay for a battery and be on my way, but the owner wanted to chat and asked me if other watches had stopped working.

"Well, yes…many…all of them actually," I responded.
"Do they stop working within months?" asked the watchmaker.
"Yes, they do," I replied.

"It's not your watches, mate. It's you. You have too much electricity and that damages the analog mechanism inside the watch. Do your digital watches last longer?" He asked.

"Yes, until their plastic straps break," I said. He handed back the watch to me and we carried on with some small talk around the topic. All the time my mind was beginning to explode with crazy ideas; superpowers being harnessed. The grin appearing on my face could only be masked by my long mustache!

I took the watch home and told my brother the bad news. It wasn't the non-existent battery or the quality of the watch, but the wind-up mechanism had failed, all due to my newly found superpowers. I am sure my family probably thought I had dropped it or done something to it, but the story was a good one. The *Dhillon's* of Tipton had their own Uri Geller!

How does an analog metallic, mechanical device like a wristwatch stop working? Are there geopathic zones affecting the interaction between the vibrational frequencies of myself (electromagnetic energy) and the energy of the metallic encased watch? Am I creating a massive amount of magnetic energy? If so, maybe I can get "off-the-grid" and simply power my electrical devices... or my electric-powered vehicle. Or is it my manation or vibrational field affecting electronics and delicate mechanisms? Jokes aside, whatever it is, it's electrical in nature and helps to support my overriding argument that WE are not this body, but the energy that is dwelling within and that radiates over twenty feet in diameter around you (your aura). So much for your so-called 2 feet (60.96 cms) of personal space! What might be its source? Just like the raindrops of a downfall are the evaporating water from the large body of waters, the source of our energy is not the energy microns, but the body of the source is the real U - the cosmic energy we all idolize and worship through the means of physical deities or scriptures. Without this energy, we are nothing but empty pods made from the five elements.

Our heart generates the largest electrical energy field in the body. Without its pulsating, rhythmic beat, and its life-giving oxygenated and nutrient-rich blood, this undoubtedly complex machine resembles an automobile that is standing lifeless in a wrecking yard. Our nervous system requires electricity to send signals throughout the body and to the brain. Why is it that the heart is the only organ in our body that pulsates? Why is it that we are certified as clinically dead only when the heart has stopped beating? The great eastern traditions all describe the body as being a mere vehicle in which to navigate through your time on earth. You are not the vehicle, but the driver - a part of the energy source within. We all are energy and the pulsating forcefield radiates out from our bodies with such strength that it can be sensed over one-and-a-half lengths of a classic Volkswagen Beetle. All life forms carry their own energy fields.

---

*For centuries, the art of dowsing has been used by man across the globe to locate groundwater and buried metals (both have an electrical vibration frequency). Today, it is used by many multinational companies to help locate underground running streams, buried regional water, and sewage piping.

It is what unites us all together. It is what makes us universally ONE.

The Creation is in the Creator, and the Creator is in the Creation

"khaalik khalak khalak meh khaalik"

– Guru Granth Sahib, page 1350

I recently read something that made me want to try out an experiment, to shed light on some quantum physics research currently underway. Scientists are testing out the hypothesis that we are not made up of solid matter, but are composed of energy (quantum physics is a contemporary science, but the argument that we are energy and not solid matter has been spoken about by ancient *Rishi's* in India and the likes of Socrates in Europe thousands of years ago. But Newtonian physics of the seventeenth century, the cornerstone of western science, theorized that there is only matter and nothing else). As one goes deeper into the workings of an atom, you would actually find energy waves and no solid matter, like invisible force fields that are emitting waves of electrical energy.

My personal research had me making a set of dowsing rods from a pair of wire clothes hangers. *Dowsing or divining rods were traditionally made from a forked branch, preferably from a hazel

---

*The dowsing device can be Y-shaped or L-shaped. They can be made from various materials including Hazel, Willow, Peachtree twigs for the Y-shaped and Copper, Glass, and Steel, for the L-shaped rod.

tree, though willow and peachtree branches were also accepted. The metal ones worked well enough for my experimental purposes. The hangers are cut, bent, and twisted into the shape of a horizontal letter 'L'. The short sides are placed into drinking straws to allow the metal portions to move freely.

Every molecule and atom in the human body has its own unique vibrational frequency. Geopathic zones affect the interaction between these frequencies, causing electric and magnetic distortions, thus creating an imbalance when you enter that space. You may think that it's lofty ideas to be exploring with wire clothes hangers and plastic straws. However, I proceeded undaunted.

You place a rod in each hand while they act as external antennae that moves inwards when you think and feel something negative, and outwards when you think and feel something positive. This isn't witchcraft or magic. I found that it simply moves without any conscious effort on my part. Every time I directed my attention to a specific person or thing in my vicinity, the metal wands worked their way to that particular direction. The trick I found is that you must think of that person, place or object and then feel that thought deep within your core. As soon as you do this, you're proving that your thoughts are energy and that they are capable of manifesting the physical.

I carry my dowsing/diving rods - my energy meters in my laptop bag. They have been pulled out at work, at the local coffee shops, and when family and friends come over, guests are asked to hold them and think about good or bad thoughts. To date, there is nobody, absolutely nobody that hasn't been able to control them and provide a reading. There may be skeptics, but I hope that people understand the power of thoughts and feelings.

As with many things that surround spirituality and consciousness, the skeptics are many. This further strengthens the argument about how the vast majority of us are wandering the earth, lost to our true identity, not realizing who or what we really are. The cynics usually write off dowsing as merely the amplification of slight movements in the operator's hand caused by a phenomenon known as the idiomatic effect. However, open-minded individuals may allow their subconscious minds to influence their bodies without them consciously deciding to take action.

But that's exactly it. Your mind and consciousness need to take charge. Place the metal hangers in the hands of an individual who meditates, who reflects upon their daily actions, who understands that they are 100% energy, beautiful, free-flowing energy, and the dowsing/divining rods can be controlled. Flowing water creates an energy field. Flowing love or hatred also creates their own energy fields. Yet, the life and doctrines that we practice on a regular basis are geared to reflect a negative outlook on your existence when in fact, we should all be rejoicing. We concentrate on the workloads, the traffic jams, and the petty arguments instead of manifesting the little joys in our daily lives. We can always make the choice to concentrate on the ever-changing sky, the lull of flowing water, the birdsong, or a stranger's smile; this is really up to us. Positive or negative energy. So, the creator is energy and we are energy? Then how do we communicate with him/her/it? Through our thoughts or actions? But the average individual can have 50,000 thoughts a day! How do you go through this vast number of thoughts and extract your prayers and wants? You must focus on them.

The ritual of prayer and the desire to have them answered has led to the monopolizing of one's own internal communication system. Instead of learning how to communicate with the cosmic energy around us, we have been told to submit to a higher power, using a particular set of practices in order to communicate with the said power. Organized religion teaches us that to communicate with our maker, a one-on-one isn't easy.

The main goal is to push aside every individual communication and make it the exclusive domain of the institution.

Your life is meant to be filled with abundance. We have been given the tools to be fulfilled and complete in every way. We are not here to suffer. We're here to grow and to reach our maximum potential. The full human potential journey is for each of us to embark upon. It doesn't matter on which geographical patch of land you were born. It doesn't matter if your patch of land is deemed to be a 1st world or a 3rd world country. Materialism and economic dominance is not the measurement used when we talk about abundance. Abundance must be of the mind and it must be felt deep within. What is materialistic abundance if you are emotionally sick or depressed? Pick up any magazine at your local grocery store, or listen to a morning TV or radio show; the lives of many of the rich and famous are rife with sad stories of their relationships, their substance abuse, and general depressive attitudes. They are all too common because financial success or celebrity status does not equate to inner wealth. If you have not conversed with the great cosmic energy, the real U, then you do not know that you are active energy. You are as free as a bird. You are not a prisoner of your body, the paparazzi or the outer world. The rich and famous are easy examples because they are low-hanging fruit. Let's face it, we don't have to look too far to see that we're unnecessarily attached to weights that drag us down, instead of allowing us to soar, as is our birthright.

If science confirms a theory, then the masses have no choice but to accept it as fact. If science leads the way for something to be investigated, measured and confirmed, then we have to take notice because we have proof. The evidence demands it. Millions of words make up the mythologies and stories that are found in religion. However, these stories sometimes cover up the actual message. The essence of the original philosophy has either been diluted or become completely unrecognizable. Why do many look at religion with a skeptical eye? Even though there are so many to choose from, many Gen-X, Millenials, Gen-Zers do not believe in organized religion. Why? The rituals and doctrines meted out by various clergy are like ball bearings in a metal canister. When you rattle it, it certainly is loud! However, the vessel itself can be somewhat empty. When the opportunity for growth and connection is removed from the individual and replaced with empty rituals and doctrines, then the individual is nothing more than that metal canister. Empty with only a few things rattling around, and making a lot of noise.

We are all connected, all of us; plant and animal life. We are all electromagnetic energy in our true nature. We occupy these shells but when our time is over, we simply move on. In the animal world, spiders have mechanoreceptor organs called slit sensilla; these allow them to sense minute mechanical strains on their exoskeleton, thereby giving them a sense of what is around them. They are able to sense their physical environment and any threat within it. Pigeons can detect the earth's magnetic field; all pigeons have a small amount of iron content in their beak and skeletal frame, which acts like a compass to help them navigate with incredible accuracy over great distances. This sense is called magnetoreception. Sharks, jellyfish, the unusual-looking platypus, and snakes, the vast majority of the animal kingdom uses the energy and its magnetic fields to help them survive, communicate, and thrive.

Dogs, cats, tropical birds, and fish are common household pets that satisfy any emotional void we might feel. There are stories of completely wild animals bonding with lost children that they rescued and cared for. Stories proliferate tales of animals possessing a sixth sense in knowing the thoughts and feelings of humans.

How do animals transfer information to one another? Scientists and researchers talk about modes of communication, which include visual, auditory, olfactory, electro, touch, and thermal. In recent times, many of the accepted understandings of how animals communicate is being rewritten, as more and more is being understood.

Telepathy, from the ancient Greek word *tele* meaning 'distant' and *pathos* meaning 'feeling, is the transmission of information from one being to another without any physical interaction. Any dog owner can confirm that they are convinced that their pets know the timing of their owner's arrival, even when the arrivals are staggered and unplanned. A friend told me about her own experiment with her German Shepherd. She found that if she wordlessly visualized what she wanted to convey, her dog understood and completed the task in the same way as when she gave the spoken command! Now, how is this not the same as thinking and feeling what you want to materialize? Examples of our energy being used for communication should really not come as a shock. It's the primal way of communicating. As languages and the spoken word became more prominent, maybe we lost the art of communicating through reading each other's energy...

Try This...

On your daily commute to school or work, try eliminating

the distraction of choice, leaving the car stereo/radio off and headphones in your coat pocket. Don't play or listen to podcasts/music on your commute; instead, try and spend time reflecting on your thoughts. Contemplate on our thoughts and actions from the previous day. Did any of those actions generate negative energy for somebody else or yourself? How can you prevent the growth of negative actions…by changing your attitude, thinking, and mindset? The technique to do so requires you to reflect hourly, preferably than just daily or weekly. Now, contemplate how you would like the day to have unfolded or the next day to evolve. At this point in the physical commute/journey within, you are probably close to getting to your final destination. Have no fear; use the 'end of the day' commute ritual to continue contemplating. Thoroughly and thoughtfully study your mental list and how you like the day to unfold. What would you like to achieve, to gain? How can you grow as a person? How can you make life better for those around you? Be a source of energy *to* others, don't be the extractor of energy *from* others!

Energy Vampire

They don't have pasty white powered skin, satin cloaks or large canine teeth that leave small puncture holes into the part of the body they seek to extract your life-giving-blood; no, they look just like you and me. Yet, after spending any amount of time with them, you feel drained – zapped of energy. Yes, you've been in the company of an energy vampire. Their conversations and general aura invisibly connect into your energy storage, leaving you feeling flat and in much need of some umph! You may need to decide here… If you continue to engage with that individual, you will leave the rendezvous feeling negative towards that individual. It is recommended that you prepare for what is about to follow or choose not to keep company with such individuals (assuming you cannot help them, of course). I have found that most of these energy vampires are oblivious of their condition and go through life with a dwindling list of victims!

Grey Cloud Grabber

Another type of individual that you may meet on your daily travels is the grey cloud grabber. You know, the ones who always want to carry the world's weight on their tiny shoulders, life is always, always a challenge for them, nothing ever seems to be correct, the glass half empty types. And when there's a break in the dark grey clouds, and shafts of strong positives sunlight energy beat down upon them, well they can't have that now can they, no, no, no. They would instead reach out and grab another grey cloud - like pulling the strings of a kite – until is sits above them, pissing down with cold rain. God forbid that their daily routine of complaining about something, or another might have been broken. For them, negative energy must feel like a wet quilt draped heavily over their head and shoulders. Like the energy vampires, be careful with these types of individuals. I have found that rarely are you able to change their attitude towards life. Why? Because change must manifest from deep within the individual. Focus on providing support around their inner journey – for them to know themselves, the real U, indeed in the most naked way. Only then can change manifest. The grey cloud grabbers seem to be happy to be suffering from some form of physical, mental, or social misfortune, and only THEY can begin rectifying the predicament.

The Giver

Then some provide you with much needed and welcomed energy – peace of mind, comfort, reassurance; I called them the givers. In their presence, you feel calm and content. Do they glow? Do angelic beings play golden harps over their heads? I don't know, but I do know that they can reset your energy levels, sometimes for a short period, other times for a lifetime - knowing or unknowingly. And unlike being in the presence of energy vampires, you will feel your battery pack being charged up. Life and all that it brings or throws your way - the high and the low points - all will seem digestible, when in the presence of a giver.

The givers typically provide support unconditionally. Some are tapped into the energy source within; others do this because it *feels* right. The objective should always be, to be on the inner journey. Beyond having the mindset of a giver, you begin to understand the importance of *The Three Houses*. The last house – the global village we all reside in, is created through contribution – this whole journey is ONLY about giving!

As I mentioned earlier, the average human has over 50,000 thoughts a day, and the clear majority of them are recycled from the previous days. Why is it important for you to know this gigantic number? Really, 50,000 thoughts a day. That's 2,083 thoughts per hour if you take into consideration the full 24 hours in a day, but let's be realistic. We are awake for approximately 16 hours a day, so you have approximately 3,125 recurring thoughts per hour. That's over 50 thoughts a minute! Communication with that energy within, and around every living thing, is possible. We need to paralyze the thoughts that do not benefit us and select what we want and desire. We need to listen to ourselves and dare I say, by doing so, we are listening to the sounds and vibrations of the cosmic energy we pay homage to! It seems simple enough, yet it requires perpetual effort.

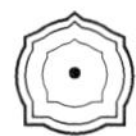

Randomness:

YOUR THOUGHTS...

THE AVERAGE PERSON HAS THIS MANY THOUGHTS A DAY.

50,000

EVERY WAKING HOUR, THIS IS HOW MANY THOUGHTS RUN THROUGH YOUR MIND.

3,125

HOW MANY THOUGHTS PER MINUTE?

52

IN ORDER FOR DREAMS TO MATERIALIZE YOU HAVE TO FOCUS ON THOUGHTS.

HOW MANY TIMES A DAY, HOUR, MINUTE ARE YOU DOING THIS?

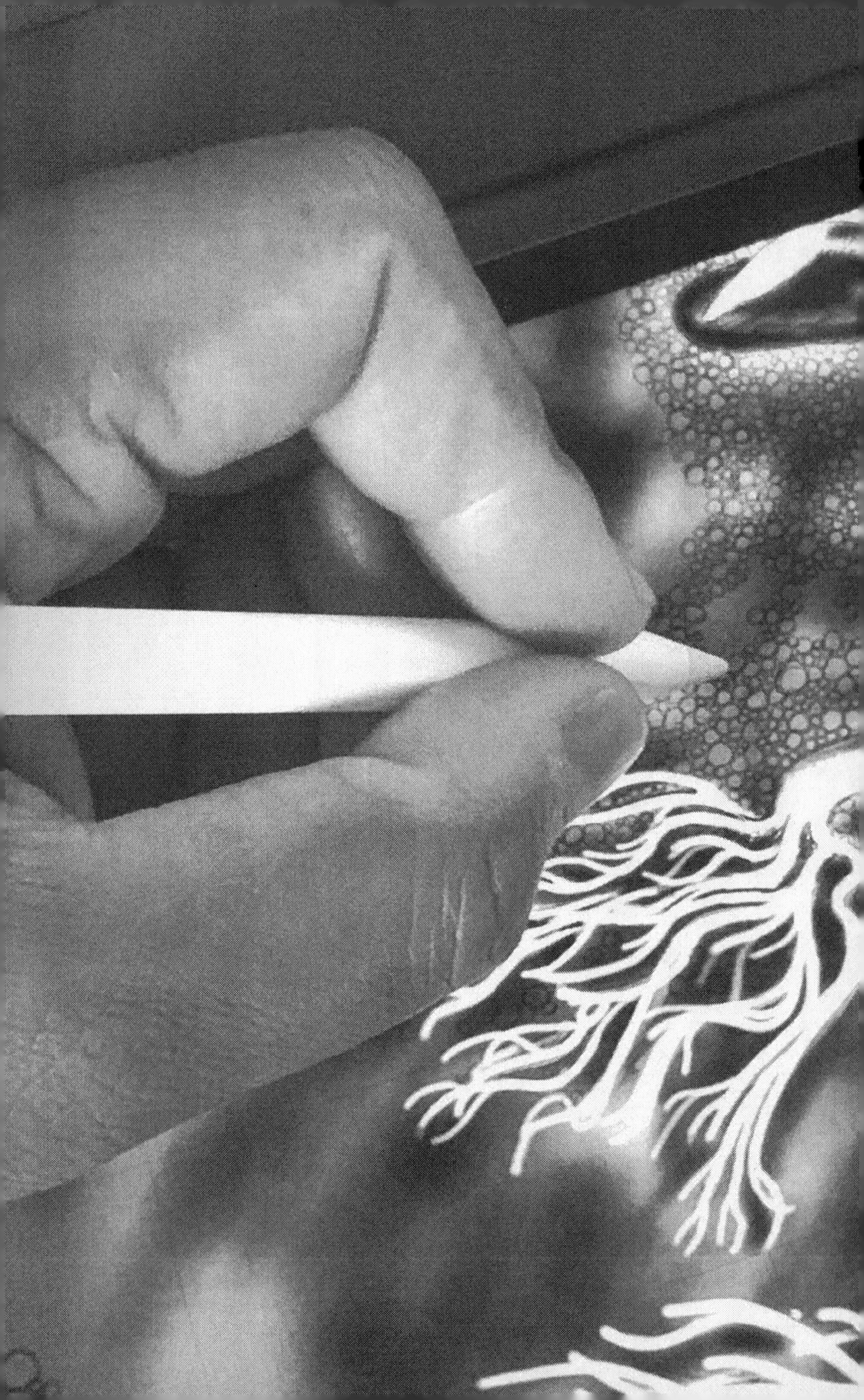

CHAPTER 15
Designing a Happy Life

I like to describe my professional self as a "designer" gone wrong. I was trained as an industrial designer, but I would consider myself as a problem solver for the past decade. It really doesn't matter what kind of problem it may be, I simply engage my design-thinking to figure things out, be that engineering issues, or emotional/social situations, by being empathetic and analytical, to the problem.

So, how does one solve one of life's most important equations, and design a happy life? The textbook description of design-thinking describes the following five stages:

1. **Empathise** (Develop a deep understanding of the challenge).
2. **Define** (Clearly articulate the problem you want to solve).
3. **Ideate** (Brainstorm potential solutions; select and develop solution).
4. **Prototype** (Design a prototype to test all or part of your solution).
5. **Test** (Engage in a continuous short-cycle innovation process to continually improve your design).

Start by **Empathizing** with yourself, learn to listen to your inner voice. Question yourself; why do I feel content? What makes me feel unhappy? I have all these positive things in my life, but why do I focus on the negative? These are all the questions we have to ask ourselves in order to understand our inner challenges. Once these questions are answered, you begin to recognize those elements of your personal life that are problematic. You identify your needs and what you want to solve - this is the **defining** step. Next, comes brainstorming (**ideate**); you have already stepped outside of your normal behavioural patterns and asked yourself some difficult questions. Now it is time to come up with solutions - what can you do to change how you feel? Come up with ideas and choose what works for you personally. It may be writing a journal every day; it may be quiet time to reflect on how your day went; it may be to express gratitude to all the good things in your life - decide what you want to do and then put it to the test. Make a list and do it regularly if needed. If there is one thing that I have realized, is that most problems, especially within our daily lives, are usually a collection of small nonsensical issues that have not been resolved, and begin to compile into an encyclopedia sized situation. Internalizing sensory signals and scenarios can keep you trapped. Changing what we take in through our senses can also help us feel much better.

The next step is to try out different methods and techniques for fixing the situations; **prototype** the solution and implement it. If it fails, try the next version, and then the next one. Be ready to pivot and move on trying alternative solutions. Once you notice an improvement in the current situation, be prepared for the future…how? **Test** yourself daily. Educate your mind and recognize your thoughts; if you want to change your life, then change your thoughts. Use your past experiences as a learning guide, both the good and bad situations that you have gone through. Now rinse and repeat!

What is 'happy'?

We had over 300 hundred employees at my previous place of

employment. A few years ago, our receptionist, who observes every individual that walks into the global head office, stopped me one day and said, "Of all the people that work here, you seem to be the only one that always seems happy and polite, and I know that life can have its ups and downs, but you always seem to have an air of care and compassion about you. I don't know what it is, but I felt that I should tell you."

"Well thank you. That really means a lot to me," I said... and it did!

I had already begun working on this book and feelings of self-doubt and critical voices within were asking the question: Am I capable of completing such a huge undertaking? Do I have enough knowledge to share? The electromagnetic energy and the secret to living a blessed life means to use the universe. Whenever there is a problem and you need answers, you simply put it out there. Ask the universe, the cosmic energy force to assist you. Share it with the greater you. I do that constantly; it helps me to walk around with a smile on my face; an air of contentment, and when challenged with tasks that seem out of my league, I simply do the same again - have faith in the energy source and myself, which allows me to stay happier. Some may argue and challenge this point by stating that this happier-for-longer is simply confidence gained from previous experiences, lessons learned from past situations, rather than tapping into electromagnetic energy. Then why are some people not able to learn, to grow from their experiences? Why are some of us intent on walking around with a dark cloud over our heads, and if the cloud moves on, they look for a surrogate one to highjack. Their outlook on life is so gloomy and negative that a lifetime of learned lessons and good experiences will never help them see life for what it is: magnificent and beautiful.

We have a limited time on this spinning rock called Earth. We are born, we will die, and what happens in between is called life. How we live that life will determine whether we can say that we have been happy or not.

Let's look at the roster of emotions that stand to prevent you from feeling happy. Pessimism, resentment, and anger are but a few. They can all be clustered together and be called Negative Thinking. Happiness is a regiment made up of empathy, serenity, gratitude, and transient experiences that lead to prolonged states of contentment. Together, they embody "Positive Thinking".

The emotions that lead to happiness don't necessarily echo societal values. Being wealthy does not guarantee happiness. Being poor does not mean that you're unhappy. In 2013, whilst I was on a trade mission to India, I had the opportunity to meet with a friend who's a Bollywood actor in *Mumbai.* As we drove from my hotel to another location for lunch, we were caught in mid-day traffic. Those that know *Mumbai*, know very well its traffic nightmares. As we sat in standstill traffic, about to merge onto a roundabout with a fly-over to my right, I glanced over and noticed a lady sitting cross-legged with a baby in her arms on the ground; she sat under the fly-over on red brick rubble, in the shadow of the large concrete structure providing some protection over her. The image resembled an info-commercial for adopting children from the less privileged countries, but she had this radiant smile on her face, an air of contentment, and bliss that one would never have expected. My automatic assumption chip would have certified her as being sad, depressed, and not content. I felt that it couldn't have been further from the truth I stared at her for what felt like eons...I put my window down to try and connect with her energy. She alone broke ALL social stereotypes. This was an experience that challenged my inner assumptions. See, it's not the physical, as was mentioned earlier, but the non-physical, the real U that determines the state of mind. Layered over is your attitude towards your environment that dictates an immediate response. It's your attitude that controls how well your day is going. I mentioned the fact that we all have a limited amount of time here on earth, and one must make a daily choice on the outcome of that day. It's a conscious decision that you have to make, and then keep making.

The happiness of your life depends upon the quality of your thoughts.

- Marcus Aurelius, Meditations (121 - 180)

One of the many things that I have learned from Cindy is making sure you are only YOU. That sounds nonsensical, but let me explain; I found that I had multiple layers of me at my disposal. Depending upon which situation I was in, and who within my ecosystem, I would appear with the perceived face for my audience. Acting in a certain way with elders from my community versus friends at work who might have been predominantly younger. These layers of personality in fact became multiple coatings that were concealing the REAL me

.

"…*Waits at the window, wearing the face that she keeps in a jar by the door. Who is it for?*"

The 1966 Beatles *Revolver* album featured the song titled, *Eleanor Rigby* on side one. For those of you that didn't grow up in the 1960s, 70s, and 80s with records and cassettes, both mediums held music on two sides. With records you could lift the needle inwards on the rotating record, choosing to play the next song or simply skipping a few. With cassettes, it was all about fast-forwarding and stopping to see if you have reached the song you want to listen to.

This particular song for me has always been a fan favourite. Not only because of the lyrics but also the general melody and sound. As I listened to the song, I began to mentally dissect the lyrics, visualizing the locations and situations, taking myself on a three-dimensional journey. I have always seen the character, Eleanor, standing in the porch of her 1930s period style semi-detached house; the brick walls shoot up from the ceramic tiled floor, up to a set of windowpanes, some of which have a small stain glass motif to help cast colour, even on the many grey days Britain is known for. The three-faced entrance to her house also shares its floor space with potted plants, her tidy little shoe rack, and a tall black elegant umbrella leaning against the inner porch wall. Next to her umbrella on the right-hand side of this vestibule is a large mason jar with no lid, filled with many faces, personality faces! When Sir Paul McCartney was asked in an interview, he said that the lyric refers to a jar of cold cream which was applied to her face, to make her look younger. The song highlights the daily lives of two lonely individuals (Father McKenzie being the other), a ballad about lonesomeness, and quite possibly, an early beacon for mental health awareness. So don't keep jars by your door full of your faces...YOU will forget who U really are!

We need to let our real-self shine 24/7. There should be no need for a superficial you! Don't cloak your emotions, rather challenge them internally and then let your inner self radiate. Your inner vessel should always be half full rather than half empty, and let the world know that too. How do we achieve that? You maintain a full glass rather than empty, by choosing the right environment or choosing to be surrounded by people that increase your probability of being happy! Fall

Illustration 20: Always half full
by Rashpal Singh Dhillon (1966)

in love frequently; I don't mean change partners, no, fall in love with beauty, wonder, and nature that surrounds you. This is the feeling of engaging in random acts of kindness. Love what you are doing and do what you do with love.

I would have to state that pursuing a happy life is the single most important journey that every human being should take. Knowing what *really* makes you happy, in the context of this world that we live in, is your destiny, and being able to understand when you might have taken the wrong route is absolutely key. Today, psychologists and doctors tell us about the brain and research on happiness. Drugs are prescribed for those that are depressed. Is there an alternative? Maybe. Quiet time (The Art of Doing Nothing = Meditation). When one begins to peel away all those inner layers of falsity and illusion of self, and instead come to terms with the real U. We don't need stimulation all of the time. Our lives are connected to technology for multiple hours of the day…we all need a break; we all need some solitary confinement of oneself.

The word meditation seems to carry too much baggage and is also over-used and controlled by too many groups. It's also over-prescribed and seems like everyone you talk to today is meditating, but are they really? To help lessen the perceived baggage around the word meditation, let's refer to it as quiet time. Imagine sitting comfortably in your bed, propped up with pillows and a nice quilt covering those extremities of your body you wish to have covered. You can sit with your legs stretched out in front of you, and your arms can sit comfortably in your lap. Lights can be off or dimmed down, whatever works for you, and then close your eyes and begin with focusing on your breathing.

Here in the West, we don't really know how to truly breathe! We tend to take short shallow breaths that barely pass the upper chest cavity area. Have you ever tried taking a deep breath as you focus on your navel area, feeling your breath right there? Quiet time, simple breathing exercises, and focusing on the breath will allow you to begin the journey. When you sit, your mind will be inundated with thoughts; your exterior environment might be calm and possibly quiet, but the *mental* chatter of thoughts coming/going will or should make you realize that you have to work on your quiet time. Simplifying meditation: let the thoughts come, and then let them go. Acknowledge them, but don't dwell on them. This phase will take some time to master. I found the procedure of acknowledging coming and going thoughts relaxing in itself.

Quiet time should be used as a daily tool to help you understand yourself, it's self-therapy. I cannot understand myself from within, unless I remove the layers of experience that I have witnessed, and then assumed that these encounters are ME. They are not me! Like the sculptor and her clay, she may place small pieces of clay onto the original form; we are that original form, the clay is the layers of experiences, good or bad that have layered our original essence, and we, therefore, think of our current form to be ME, when in fact, the original form is someone else. Quiet time will help to remove these layers.

In order for happiness to become your natural state, you have to put in the effort to make it so. That effort has to be greater than the sum of negativity that we are bombarded with daily.
The final thing I would like to share on designing a happy life is to plant these seeds; live in the NOW, serve others around you, and always put material possessions into perspective.

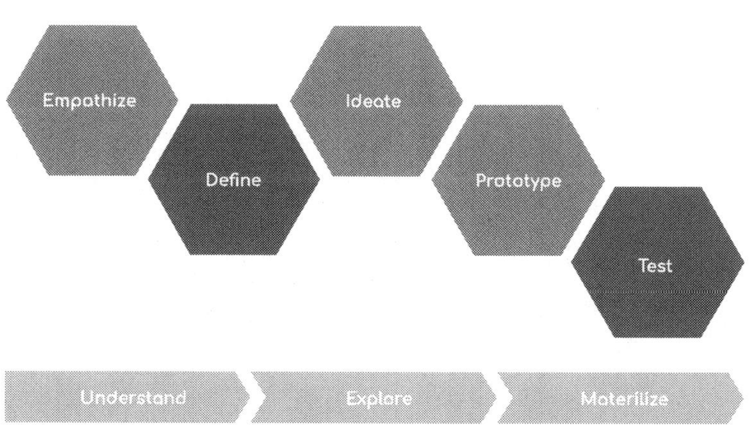

Illustration 21: Design Thinking
by Kulbir Colin Singh Dhillon

Randomness:

1ST OF SIKH ORIGIN TO ARRIVE IN CANADA (PRINCE VICTOR ALBERT JAY DULEEP SINGH)

Victor Albert Jay Duleep Singh was born in the summer of 1866, the first son of Maharaja Duleep Singh and Maharani Bamba. He was christened by his Godmother, Queen Victoria, at a private chapel in Windsor.

On September 18th, 1888 Prince Victor left Liverpool harbour on the Steamship Caspian. It set sail for Halifax, Nova Scotia, Canada, and arrived on September 30th, 1888.

Just twenty-one years after the birth of the nation (The 1867 British North America Act establishing Canada as a new country when we know it belongs and has always belonged to the Indigenous people of North America!), the grandson of the Lion of Punjab, Maharajah Ranjeet Singh, became the first of Sikh origin to live on the shores of Canada!

In 2016, I embarked on a journey to tell the story of Prince Victor. The writing and creation of the documentary film, titled, The Lion that Lost his Roar, took my film crew and me to Eton College, Cambridge University, Sandhurst Military College, Paris, and Nice in France, and onto Nova Scotia, Canada. As I wove the threads of his life story together, what materialized was a tragic tale of a young man, who could have been the Maharajah of the Sikh Kingdom.

For more information, please visit http://victorduleepsingh.com

Image: Documentary Poster. Designed by Lucas Lopez & Kulbir Colin Singh Dhillon

THE PRINCE VICTOR ALBERT JAY DULEEP SINGH STORY

1ST OF SIKH ORIGIN TO ARRIVE IN CANADA

THE LION THAT LOST HIS ROAR

A FILM BY KULBIR COLIN SINGH DHILLON

victorduleepsingh.com

SIKH HERITAGE MUSEUM OF CANADA PRESENTS "THE LION THAT LOST HIS ROAR"

WRITTEN & DIRECTED BY KULBIR COLIN SINGH DHILLON CO-PRODUCED BY SIKHLENS DIRECTOR OF PHOTOGRAPHY DREW MOE

EDITED BY SUNNY TAMBER ART DIRECTOR KULBIR COLIN SINGH DHILLON GRAPHICS BY LUCAS LOPEZ

SCRIPT EDITED BY MITA HANS PRODUCED BY THE SIKH FOUNDATION OF CANADA SOUND BY CINEVERSE

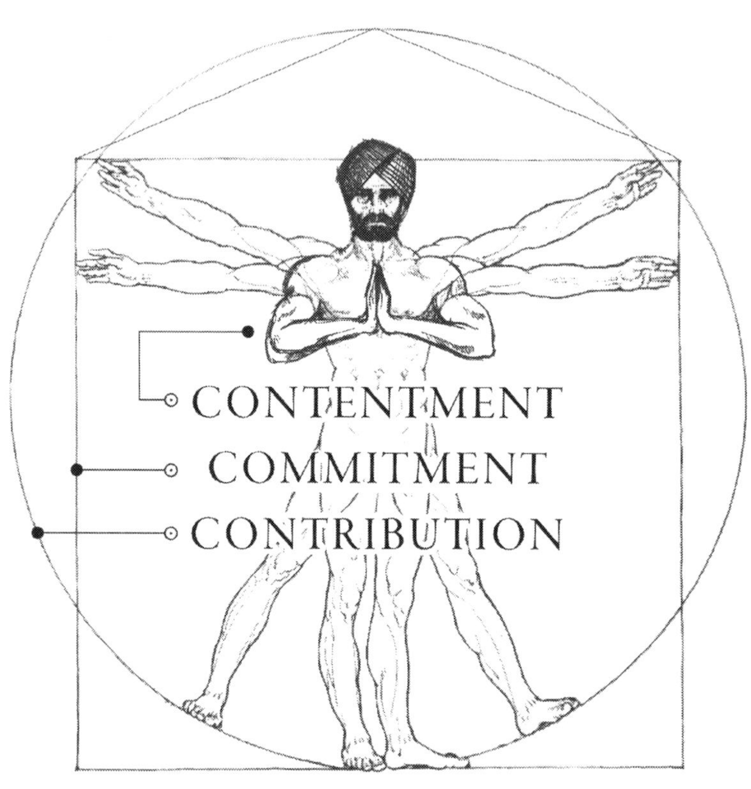

Illustration 22: The Three Houses;
Contentment, Commitment, Contribution
by Kulbir Colin Singh Dhillon

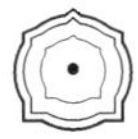

CHAPTER 16

The Three Houses

The year was 2015, and I was in my mid-forties. Life has seen occasions and circumstances similar to many of you, and possibly alien and strange to others. The highs and lows, the happy and challenging times have all carried me to this point in time, and guess what, I believe wholeheartedly that I live a blessed life because of all of it! But how so, how has the bullying, prejudice, the seeking of a spiritual path not shaken my resolve? I believe ALL the events in my life, the macro and micro pains, and joyous occasions have moulded me externally, but most importantly and internally, into ME.

So, how do I explain this to friends, colleagues, and those that simply ask? How do we unearth one's practices and make them universally applicable? I do this by taking the nectar from the fruit of my life, and label it, *The Three Houses* (Contentment, Commitment, and Contribution). A simple set of guidelines that one needs to apply into their everyday lives. This chapter is both the title of my book and a pivotal part of my life's journey.

Contentment: The World Health Organisation (WHO) estimates that one in four people in the world is affected by a mental disorder at some point in their lives. Commitment: 45% of all marriages in North America, end in divorce. Contribution: There's not enough support being given to those in need in both your life and mine. These three "C's" are my three houses!

My personal rendition of Leonardo da Vinci and the Roman architect, Vitruvius. A Vitruvian man was chosen to describe the three houses. This globally recognized image brings together all the 3 elements: The human, the home, and the circle depicting the spinning rock upon which we all reside. Its visual simplicity compliments the humble message of contentment, commitment, and contribution.

The first of the three houses is you, your human abode. One must live with contentment inside this dwelling in order to have a truly wonderful, and blessed life. The second is the house we all plan on making or living within, surrounded by your "loved ones". In order for this house to succeed, one must be committed: to your partner, to your children, to your parents etc. Extract that commitment and we all know what happens to that house... it falls apart. The final house is the planet earth, and for this house to prosper, contribution must play a major part in your vocabulary. Giving back is paramount for this house to succeed, and your contribution will only strengthen the other two houses.

I see a person as a human shell, flexible yet encasing our core base of contentment. Here, everything is in harmony with itself, all intact. This is our first house, the home where nothing exists outside of ourselves. This is the house where our spirituality and creativity share an interstellar void. Our capacity for love and anger lives side by side, sometimes intertwined, and we decide how much emphasis we apply to each and how much time is spent visiting those inner personality realms.

For me, my contentment lies in my conviction, in my love for my family, in my work and creativity. I draw contentment from the silence of mind, the contemplation of action, and allow it to grow and penetrate within to where it is most needed.

Surrounding this individual dwelling is the house that we all wish to reside in, to build, and to make into a home. This abode is your safe haven, it's your castle that is illuminated by not just mere electric bulbs, but the radiant energy of loved ones that reside alongside you. This house is called commitment, and its multi-layered stage in one's life is of practical value both at home and in the workplace. Commitment manifested itself almost immediately in my life through the act of building a beautiful life with my family, in creating this abode through harmony and healthy energy. A physical space where visitors can come for refreshments and leave fulfilled!

The third house is the house of contribution. It is the orb that carries everyone and encompasses everything. The alpha and the omega of all that we put out into the Omniverse and what it, in turn, provides back to all of us. This is the outer layer of the space, the cosmic garden party where we stand admiring the flowers and look inward to gain perspective on the complete space.

We decide which building materials of creation we are going to bring into developing and strengthening the structure of this house. You want to bring an attitude like straw material, then be prepared to be unstable within and get blown away, just like James Orchard Halliwell-Phillipps fairy tale, *The Three Little Pigs*. Your stability of mind and inner strength will be the platform for serving and contributing to this global village we all live in.

You are a part of the cosmic energy force and it makes itself known to you when you contribute selflessly. In *Sikhism*, it's called Selfless Service (*Nishkam Seva*). The only gain is spirituality with an undertone of humility. One might ask, how is humility a gain? Humility in the individual will allow them to support an attitude of contribution; to be humble. It also interconnects with one's compassion and love of oneself and others.

The three dwellings encompass us all. You cannot escape them, you might try to ignore them, but these houses are connected to one another, just like in a multi-directional relationship. You might focus on one more than the other, but focus on them all and the magic begins. Let me take you deeper into each abode.

Contentment

This house is the most important, and yet, the most challenging to live in. How many of us like to spend quality time alone without any distractions within ourselves? Can you go through your morning routine without any background noise? Can you go to school, or to work without listening to music or your favourite podcast, but instead just listening to your thoughts? How many of us are happy to be alone? Our lives are a collaboration of visual, audible, emotional distractions. The 'silence of mind' is transcribed as a remedy in the East, but in the Western hemisphere, it is misunderstood to be punishment, i.e., sending your child to their room as a measure of discipline, instead of teaching your loved ones the benefits of silence. You should want to spend quality time with the most important person in your life, YOU!

It's a scary thought, right? It's hard to listen to yourself, acknowledge your fears, and be glaringly honest with your own internal responses. It's more than scary, it can be downright terrifying! This is why we don't attempt to try this. Solitude is seen as a punishment. What do we tell a child who is misbehaving? Stand in the corner, work alone outside in the corridor, or you cannot talk with anyone! How do we punish criminals who misbehave in the prison system? We put them in solitary confinement. What do we call people who do not fit into our social circles? Loners. As a society, we have labelled quiet time as a negative thing. We fear being alone and listening to our internal dialogue. We dread closing our eyes and sitting still. When in fact we need to listen to the voices that challenge and question our actions and responses. You may not like what you hear, but don't ignore it. Contentment within happens when you peel away those layers of falsity around us; remove those masks. We tell ourselves lies and ignore the need to be brutally honest with ourselves and our actions. How do we help reverse this process and create an environment where we can begin to listen to ourselves? Quiet time is one of the answers.

As you begin to enjoy quiet time and it no longer feels like licking a river stone and expecting to be rewarded with a flavour, the inner journey can lead you in multiple directions, one being contemplation, which is critical for discovering contentment within. Contemplate on your hourly, daily actions. Was I right to have said this, to have done that? Be critical and create a wanting for self-improvement. If this aspect is missing and you have no want for self-improvement, then just lay your head down on your pillow and hit the sack! There has to be a want to correct one's words and actions, to challenge one's ego (*Hankar*). The more you challenge yourself for self-improvement, the more content you will begin to feel. At our essence, I strongly feel that we are all good-natured beings. It's the layers and layers of personal, social, religious, and political misinterpretation by us as individuals, or collectively that can add toxic layers over the purer cosmic energy that reverberates within.

Our body is the true temple of the cosmic energy we all call God. You too, the real U, resides within that temple. The soul or energy source that you are a part of is the same energy, source of the energy. As young children we spent time within ourselves, playing, creating games, and making magic happen. The imagination that provides all children with escapism becomes lost. Children can spend hours living within themselves, obviously in very small doses! As the child becomes an adult, imagination becomes but a distant memory. Yet somehow, as we got older, we began spending less and less time going inside. Rather, like an exporting company, we choose to spend all our efforts on working outside of our own borders. Be content with yourself. Your contentment will support your future commitments and contributions to the global village in which we all reside.

Practice being more content and honest with yourself. Honesty is like a radiating mirror; when there are no lies to oneself and your own relationship with yourself is always based upon 100% honesty, then the law of like attracts like and you'll be surrounded by beautiful honest creatures, making life feel like paradise on earth.

"Because one believes in oneself, one doesn't try to convince others. Because one is content with oneself, one doesn't need others approval. Because one accepts oneself, the whole world accepts him or her"

– Lao Tzu

Be thankful for what you have been provided. Enjoy this magnificent specimen of art, a truly innovative machine made from the five elements (earth, fire, water, space, wind). Be happy with who you are, begin to live an honest life, and become even more happy and content with yourself. Become your own garden, be your own library, go inside and plant those seeds of contentment, commitment and contribution. Enjoy the vast wealth of knowledge that lies within, because as I mentioned earlier, you are directly connected to the maker. Just ask and the answers will appear. Be ready to receive the messages.

Commitment

Without this pledge, a dwelling is simply occupied by individuals who share some common interests and affection for one another. Without this assurance, an employer feels compelled to thank you for your effort, but then asks you to leave with a pink slip in hand, and without this vow to oneself, you risk falling short in the pursuit of gaining all things that are possible for personal growth.

I use the simplistic line drawing of an abode to define commitment, as the outline of an androgynous figure helps to define contentment. We all must make commitments in our life's journey to create and to live a harmonious life. It requires honesty and sacrifice on your part. We are all taught at a very young age to be committed. Our parents expect this from us when it comes to the family structure, our schooling or extra curricular activities. Our learning and growth from childhood to adulthood, asks us to consider our pledge to care for the planet upon which we reside, to leave a sustainable world for the coming generations. Commitment is an integral mechanism for individuals to function in the greater society. Go into multiple applications on your smartphone and you'll see an endless number of individuals that are committed to their art and dreams. There are no universal criteria to assess commitment and I think we all know what we are agreeing to when we commit ourselves.

If you want to know the epitome of what commitment is, then let's talk about an individual, maybe someone that is not a child, sibling, or parent of yours with whom you don't have just an obligation towards, based on the nature of the relationship. This individual whom you have signed a social contract intertwined with religious connotations, and the promise of being committed for better or for worse, for richer or for poorer, and in sickness and in health. To love and cherish this person is the exemplification of unconditional commitment, something that many of us are living every day of our lives for. But let's be clear on who makes the commitment to whom. Though vows and words of an obligation are said between two individuals, in fact, it's the individual's commitments to those words that play a big part. Am I making sense? To stay committed to any cause or individual, for example, a *Soldier's Creed*, a standard by which all United States Army personnel are expected to live by, that is up to the soldier to fulfill that commitment, the army or his seniors really have no control over that soldier, though they might think they do. Similarly, both parties in a relationship, have made individual commitments to themselves to uphold the entity known as a relationship. Therefore, when I talk about commitment, I refer to an individual's pledge to themselves as being pivotal. These lessons learned around relationships, possibly around the home, subconsciously influence your tenets outside of the house, workplace, and career too.

No commitment equals the lack of an individual's depth. We all know that any substance has a short life in a shallow dish. When commitments are broken, there are emotional, physical, and economic implications that could arise. Some are short-term, others can have long-term effects on all parties. You as an individual must decide if it's worth breaking the pledge!

Each one of life's lessons, whether good or bad are like bricks and mortar that will eventually build that home, which is more than just a house. A place for you and your loved ones to feel comfortable and secure within. This is your *ashram*, your castle, your bastille - the place that you have created from the foundations of truth, compassion, contentment, humility, and love. That should be the structure of your abode. The air within your home should be oxygenated with love, the framework inside the brick structure is supported with compassion for all. The floors are laid with humility, supporting those in need, your windows are glazed with honesty, clear and transparent, and all those that reside and visit this home are left feeling content. The energy within these dwelling pierces even the thickest of skins and armour. You need these traits to be strong and flexible in order to make a house into a beautiful home.

Without these elements and actions, our house can be likened to a house of cards; an abode of individual personalities and disconnected egos, with the most fragile structure, lacking reinforced footings, foundations, and walls as personality attributes.

Like contentment, commitment has to be practiced subconsciously and like the image of an iceberg, what appears above the surface of the world's oceans, the conscious, is but a fraction of the complete entity. The subconscious labyrinth is to be explored for its depth and beauty, but not to be ignored or to become lost within. These adventures are to be had in your quiet time – when you contemplate and evaluate your thoughts and actions from that particular day – working towards self-improvement.

Like any ecosystem on the planet, we are interdependent. We can live in harmony, or in disarray within our house. We need love, compassion, truth, contentment, and humility, all balanced, each with a role to play. The sustainable advantage of being able to prosper and survive in your internal ecosystem is the ability to live a life of commitment and gratitude.

Contribution

As you carry out the daily work upon yourself, self-improvement and loving the vehicle in which you transport yourself, your contentment for yourself and who you are should be increasing, and the electromagnetic energy that is the real U begins to radiate outwards, inflicting all those around you in a positive light; like a philosopher stone!

The attitude is brought about both internally within the first house and into the place you call home, the second house. Your daily routine, to stay connected to the real U, helps to keep you in the present. The past is gone, it's no more and can sometimes be a highway of depressive potholes. The future, as bright as it ought to be, can also be laced with small doses of anxiety, tripping you up even before you live those possible experiences! The present is now. Smell those roses, enjoying the scenery all around you today, and learn to live in the NOW! Most of us struggle to be present, but when we are in the current, we can achieve the impossible. Michael Jordon, the greatest basketball player of his generation, was a grandmaster of living in the now. He might not have jumped the highest, ran the fastest, or been the most technical of players; his greatness was simply being present. Michael did not project the past into the now or near future. He, like the *Navi* characters from the movie *Avatar*, understand being present with both heart and mind.

Being present in mind is important to understanding the final house, which is the world within and around you. Putting the interest of others above your own means being vulnerable but resilient, that is why it's ideal that you work on yourself first, before contributing to society. But why in that order? Some people can spend all their lives in charitable institutions, some religious, others focused on social reform, giving all they have to a particular cause they deeply believe in, yet they are not content with themselves and their *house*. They may appear to most of us as individuals who are serene, yet internally, that same individual may be lost, disconnected, and the opposite of what charitable means. They may desire contentment and good family life, voices echoing love within the four walls of their house, and wanting it to become a home. That is why it's critical to begin with knowing oneself - for you to be brutally honest with yourself and working towards or sustaining a routine of contentment.

Like the ecosystem of a home, we need to expand that mindset and implement it, bring it into the society we live in. The question is this: Can the ideal life be one that is filled with charity and giving? Your daily objective isn't the accumulation of wealth or power, but rather to uplift those around you? Although your life goal might include doing better materialistically, this should differ from your daily objectives of self-improvement through selfless service. Contributing a monetary value towards a charity or organization that helps those in need is obviously a no-brainer.

You choose an amount that fits your budget, and an organization that you believe is providing the help and care that meets your objectives. The vast spectrum of ways in which we can and should help others is but a smile, offering a helping hand, and a strong shoulder away. Uplifting another could be a gift that just isn't comprehendible…just be prepared to step up.

This utopia has its roots within you, the change has to occur inside you first. You have to change your mindset in order for the other house scenarios to open up. Why? Because they contribute to the global village within which we reside. To contribute is to provide a part of the whole. You, as an individual, have to be a provider to the complete. Something as small as a smile can change the course upon which the person on the receiving end was possibly heading. Leave your home and feel free to throw out a smile to each person you make eye contact with. Trust me, they will see and feel the difference. Follow the smile you give with a greeting: good morning, afternoon, evening. Do all of this without looking for a response back. Rather, do this knowing you're a farmer, planting your seeds. Help make the world a better place. That starts with you on an individual level at first, then your ecosystem, spreading love and positive energy, which is truly infectious, which then escapes into the world at large. This is only one way of contributing. Do charitable service, (*seva*) helping to uplift everyone. In the Indian society, hands that don't help others are described as being dirty. Get it? Sterile hands that don't support their fellow human, their neighbour within his/her society, are impure. Why is that? That individual is still being challenged and overwhelmed by the five evils: ego, attachment, anger, greed, and lust. Be your own garden, plant your own seeds, take care of your crop, fertilize with organic and natural ingredients, protect your crop from the environment if/when required, and be prepared to harvest your crop. You need to have planted good seeds in order to live a life of harmony, one filled with compassion and all the worldly gifts and spiritual rewards of this journey we are on.

The Three Houses are to be lived in, not rented out. And when you start to live in them, your life begins to change. The peaks and valleys of daily life are still going to be there; there are no miracles, magical fixtures, or snake oil remedies, but for you to simply decide:

Would you rather have small hills or tectonic forces that have raised the earth's surface as issues? The decision is yours!

"Prolonged happiness comes from giving and not just receiving"

- Kulbir Colin Singh Dhillon

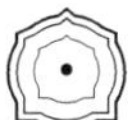

Randomness:

YOU'LL NEVER WALK ALONE

In 1978 I filled out an advertisement/coupon on the back page of a Beano comic. All I had to do was add a postage stamp, and I would receive a black wallet with a picture of Kenny Dalglish on the inside. It honestly took ages for it to arrive, I had completely forgotten that I even did this, until a piece of mail comes addressed to me. Now as an eight-year-old, you don't get a lot of mail, and I remember my Dad opening it and giving it to me, maybe I got a telling off, just in case I did something nefariously! That is when I officially became a lifelong supporter of Liverpool Football Club. Let's not forget that I jumped onto the best bandwagon in League One at that time. If we follow local 'tribal' territories, then I should have been a Baggies (West Bromwich Albion Football Club) supporter, but I chose Liverpool.

We would win everything and until the 1990s, were the dominant force in English and European footie.

I moved to Canada, and as my new life began to take shape, Liverpool became but a distant light, too far away to distract me from everyday life. When my son, Pavitar, was born and began to engage in sports as a toddler, especially football, as it reinvigorated my passion for Liverpool FC.

Today it's one of my passions and pastimes, the only television viewing that is mandatory for both my son and me. Liverpool FC legendary goalkeeper, Bruce Grobbelaar, has become a friend and refers to me as his 'Brother from another Mother.' I can only visualize the back of this titan's head, the nylon string netting on the goalposts, and tens of thousands of AC Roma and Liverpool fans holding their breath in Stadio Olimpico, Rome. Bruce does the infamous spaghetti legs move, which made Francesco Graziani miss his penalty and Liverpool FC became European Champions for the fourth time!

We are on the journey with Liverpool, the high points and many low points too. I have ink on my body, confirming that Liverpool is, in fact, my team. One thing is steadfast, and that is our song... You'll Never Walk Alone. No better sporting anthem exists on the globe today; even some Manc's will admit to that! That 'never give up' attitude is engrained in our song. The outlook on life is projected to be good and positive, even as you go through a thunderstorm of negative experiences. Still, one thing rings undoubtedly... you are never walking alone. #YNWA

Illustration 23: The Liverbird by Kulbir Colin Singh Dhillon

THE THREE HOUSES · THE THREE HOUSES

CHAPTER 17
The Finishing Touches...

Stories can be a vehicle, taking the reader on a magical and transformative journey. The black inked words create a colour palette for the mind. The voyage allows them to feel the encounters and to be a part of someone else's expressed world. Your emotions are like the keys on a piano, and each experience is the trained finger; sometimes gently and other times quite forcefully, jolting you and carrying you along a symphony of experiences. I hope *The Three Houses* have stirred all kinds of emotions deep within. I hope it gives optimism to those that feel somewhat 'less than' the sum of who you are. My personal stories were intentionally chosen, because I wanted to evoke a concerto of emotions (admiration, sadness, fear, happiness, surprise, sorrow, rage, anticipation, and joy), within in you!

I have been very fortunate to have travelled through parts of Europe, Asia, and North America. I am a people-person and a keen observer of everything within my environment. I watch the clouds move and change shape, directions, and sometimes colour, the trees and their sometimes-leafed branches, rustling in the wind, collectively all pushing in the same direction. The behaviours and idiosyncrasies of my fellow beings. I am a firm believer in the goodness of humanity. I prefer to look for the positives, rather than focusing on the negatives. This approach can sometimes be detrimental when trying to read a person, especially if the person is someone you might have to rely upon or work closely together with. The fortunate thing is that the vast majority of us are very similar. The rollercoaster type of personality with its peaks and valleys, the ups and downs seem to be commonplace. But then you come across those that don't ride the rollercoaster, instead, they cruise the rail tracks, cutting through mountainous peaks and valleys, yet somehow staying calm and content. I say learn from them! When mountain climbing, your emotions can be mentally and physically tiring, why not take the scenic route via the Orient Express.

The premise of this journey in the form of a book was to share personal experiences, some of which are painful and would give any person experiencing them a lack of confidence, a negative outlook on life, on society, and maybe the *victim mentality* syndrome. These descriptions are no breeding ground for spirituality or the search of oneself. My journey has had many guides. Some of them may not have carried the official *guide certificate* card, but they have shone a bright light in the darkness for me to find my way. For the past twenty-plus years, the years in which a boy becomes a man, when maturity begins, I have been blessed with my best friend, my lover, my partner, and wife, Cindy. We have both grown up together, taken journeys with the hope that the final destination would be sign-posted as *finding oneself.*

Well, what an adventure! Taking many stories from my life, and sharing them verbally, is one thing. Trying to bring those same stories together, include my philosophy on life and how one should live it, well, I knew it would be a gigantic undertaking. However, I knew I had to do it. The project itself was like a demon on my back, weighing me down, whispering negative comments in my ear "You'll never finish this. You're a terrible writer, and no one is going to read it!"

Those same demonic voices can be heard by every living human being, especially when you want to achieve something that may be out of your realm. Hearing them and ignoring them are galaxies apart. This book was going to be a period in my life where I overcame many obstacles because don't forget, I didn't need to write this for my career, but rather for myself and to share my journey with you. I could have simply identified the obstacles as being too large to handle, but like any bottleneck that prevents the flow of ideas, knowledge, and love, once it's been removed, only then do you see the benefit of tackling the situation.

I have been doing exactly that for many decades. I have dug deep into my inner-self and challenged it to overcome those hurdles which have either been placed there by myself or others. I am a dreamer; always have been, always will be. I want my dreams to come true. Most of them already have, some of them did not, but I didn't stop dreaming, or lose sight of where I wanted to go, rather I would ask my inner self and that cosmic energy, to simply gather my collective thoughts and set the compass in another direction. I didn't spend time looking back, wondering, "if only…", No, I maintained the course of this new voyage, always remembering where I started from, and being thankful for where I am today, and where I plan on going. Some of you might ask, if I knew things were going to be wonderful as I stood, waist-deep in a canal, with several skinheads looking down upon me? No, I did not. There were dark times and I sometimes thought that I might not get through them, but as mentioned earlier, I am a dreamer. I dreamt my reality into physicality. I dreamt away all those that wanted to harm me or to cage me.

One thing that I am not trying to do, is to push any religion or its traditions/practices down anyone's throat, rather I am sharing some of the universal guidelines that *Sikhism* is known for, and highlighting those aspects of the faith that I have practiced and feel are general in nature. I know *Sikhism* and that is why I have used examples from it.

Now that I have cleared that point, let me leave you all with some takeaways. Selfless service is key to living a wonderful life. Giving your time to help others, giving your time to help yourself - all of this helps to eradicate one's ego. Selfless service has to be recognized as the foundation stone upon which you build your dreams into some shape or form; it acts like a catalyst.
Be humble, be loving and be kind. This may sound like the *Dalai Lama's* mantra, but it's spot on. Catch yourself when you are rude, obnoxious, or unkind. Ask yourself why and reset your

thinking. This kind of behaviour harms you as much, if not more than those that you treated in that particular way.

"Holding on to anger is like grasping a hot coal with the intent of throwing it at someone else; you are the one who gets burned"

- Buddha

Find your outlet for selfless service. It doesn't have to be within the four walls of a religious institution, rather it can be done through running/walking 5km for a chosen charity, through supporting your local school, or spending time with those in need. Ask yourself what you would like to do, and then go forth and do it. Feel the inner warmth and sense of accomplishment when you do selfless service. I always compare it to giving me a 'high' without drinking alcohol or taking some kind of drug. If there is one thing you do after reading this, make that *SEVA*!

"What is the essence of life?
To serve others and to do good"

- Aristotle

Contentment, Commitment and *Contribution.* That's it.

Mic drop moment!

I am hard-pressed to challenge these three nouns, which are the drivers of a strong, loving, and successful (spiritually and materialistically) self. They are rooted in the depths of spiritual philosophies, yet simple enough to be free from the shackles of time and dogma. Be content with yourself. Work to improve and elevate your being every single day of your existence. Aim for perfection but without the worry or anticipation of knowing if you have reached the pinnacle (remember it takes just 15% more effort than usual!). Let your actions, and the quality of characters that surround you, be an understanding of whether or not you are succeeding. Commitment to oneself and your loved ones is paramount. Commitment to your employer and colleagues is also important. One does not receive recognition of work undertaken if there is a lack of commitment to one's duties. Be a committed individual, someone that others feel confident in, but most of all, be committed to your loved ones, your life partner, and family. One of Pinball's most valuable lessons was to understand that you have to be Superman in the house, not outside it...the most valuable things in life are in that abode! When contentment and commitment are housed under one roof, the energy generated within that abode is healthy and full of love, which is experienced by you and others.

"As we lose ourselves in the services of others, we discover our own lives and our own happiness"

- Dieter F. Uchtdorf

Thank you

They say it takes a village to raise a child. Well, it takes the support of a village to write a book too. I set out on this personal journey, but I knew that it would include many close friends and family members. First and foremost, I would like to thank my wife Cindy for standing beside me throughout the past twenty-six years. She has been my inspiration and motivation for continuing to improve as a person. She is my rock, and I dedicate this book to her, and to our wonderful children, *Pavitar* and *Veerah*; thank you for making our lives have purpose and meaning beyond what you both can comprehend. We want both of you to be beautiful individuals, good honest people who appreciate that it is an honour to be a good citizen of this spinning rock. I hope that one day they can read this book and understand why I spent so much time in front of my computer, and always doing those extra-curricular activities in the greater community.

My friend, Harry *Mann*, for the weekly chats on our drive to work, the multiple proofreadings and support on *Gurbani* (*Sikh* scripture content). Harry is a great friend and a scholar. To my cousin, *Jasdeep* Cook, for proofreading and not holding back with her honest feedback. To *Gurlat Singh* of Coventry, UK, my wife's cousin, but someone I feel very connected to. You challenged me to go deeper and to clarify many points, adding depth. *Mita Hans*, thank you for helping me formalize the idea of a book and being an inspirational editor on the first draft. You showed me the box, its four sides, and then said, "jump the hell out of there". Your stories, support, and your unique way of dissecting me and my world has been inspirational.

To my brother and sister-in-law, *Rajesh* and *Rani*, thank you both for always being there, and supporting me with this project. To my niece, *Kirit Shergill*, thank you for being the fastest and possibly one of the best proofreaders of all. To *Mickey Klota* and *Nipun Kasote*, thank you for helping me with the cover design, book layout, printing, and always being there…Thank you is truly not enough! To *Ruby Dhillon*, thank you for always challenging my output, and asking me to only settle for the best. To *Joss Monzon*, your artistic guidance on developing the book cover design and branding strategies have been pivotal.

Last, but definitely not least, I'd like to thank Michael 'Pinball' Clemons. Our lunchtime conversations and your persistence that I should tell my story and share my ideas is the reason this book exists today. You're a huge inspiration to me and thousands of others. You define positive electromagnetic energy; you're the embodiment of it. Thank you, my mentor and friend. I am forever indebted to you.

I had the choice to walk with a chip on my shoulder, but I chose not to. I had the choice to listen and experience only one-dimension of my faith, I chose not to. Instead, I chose to take my life's experiences and mould them into my existence today. I live a blessed life; I hope it inspires you to do the same.

Thank you!

Spring 2022

Randomness:

CIRCULAR ECONOMY FOR HUMAN DEVELOPMENT

Pavan guru

Air (Energy) is the Teacher: So long as we are alive and breathing, we are learning. We learn by listening, be it through external conversation and internally through our inner dialogue and resonance.

Pānī pitā

Water is the Father: Water is the primal energy available for all, like rain that indiscriminately showers down on all. How it is received depends on the receiver.

Mātā dharat mahat.

Earth is the Mother: Earth nurtures and provides for everyone indiscriminately. The receiver's disposition determines the fruition

So long as we are alive, we are learning, and that one primal energy sustains us all and penetrates our beings such that we grow and prosper according to our disposition.

(From researcher and historian, Harminder (Harry) Singh Mann)

About the Author

Kulbir Colin Singh Dhillon, the son of immigrants to the shores of England, headed for Canada to begin his life in the early 1990s. One of Canada's leading automotive innovation and design authorities, a globally sought-after voice on the ever-changing future of mobility, and holder multiple patents. Today, he is the Chief Technical Officer for Canada's Automotive Parts Manufacturers' Association and the creative/technical lead on Project Arrow: Canada's first electric concept vehicle project.

Outside of work, our author shares his time thoughtfully as the President of the Sikh Heritage Museum of Canada and the Chairman of the Global Syndicate for Mobility Cybersecurity. He supports these organizations through creative leadership and providing a vision for the digital Metaverse future ahead.

In 2012, Colin was awarded the Queen Elizabeth II's Diamond Jubilee Medal for his significant contributions to Canada. In 2016 our author wrote and directed the documentary film, *The Lion That Lost His Roar*, telling the tragic story of Prince Victor Jay Duleep Singh. In 2017, Colin was recognized as one of the '500 global Sikh Role Models'.

His first book, *The Three Houses*, is an accumulation of knowledge gained and created and allows him to share his life journey, along with his deep, profound philosophy for a better life for ALL people.

Colin is a devoted husband, father, son, brother, and friend. Most of all, he is happy travelling the common man's journey through life, living by his three principles: Contentment, Commitment and Contribution.
To learn more, please go to; **kcsd.ca**

Made in the USA
Coppell, TX
09 April 2022

76274894R00173